Architectural Ceramic Assemblies Workshop

Bioclimatic Ceramic Assemblies V

Architectural Ceramic Assemblies Workshop

*Edited by Laura Garófalo
and Omar Khan*

APPLIED
RESEARCH
+DESIGN
PUBLISHING   *Novato, CA*

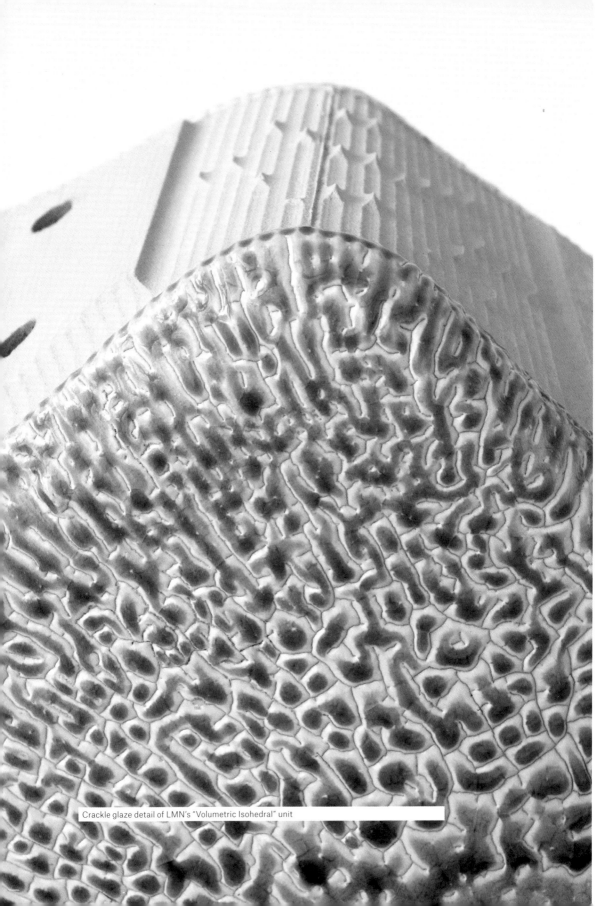

Crackle glaze detail of LMN's "Volumetric Isohedral" unit

Contents

Foreword

John Krouse

Surface detail of Smith and Gill's flowing screen units.

In many ways, the year 2020 will go down as one of the most difficult and trying years in modern history with COVID-19 imposing it's will into the world. ACAW 2020 has proven that even with a looming pandemic, our team had the fortitude to overcome setbacks and found a way to accomplish a safe and successful event. A special thanks to all the architectural teams that refused to give up and rather chose to rise to the occasion.

With minimal time to prepare and plan, we figured out a way to come together and experience a successful event through a virtual setting. Due to the skill set of some fantastic architects including Anthony Viola at Adam Smith + Gordon Gill Architecture and Mario Romero at Perkins and Will, a virtual ACAW Gallery was developed which allowed for the event to display the accomplishments of each team without an in-person gathering. Boston Valley Terra Cotta was able to assemble each of the teams' projects and submit photographs of the completed work into the virtual gallery.

Many of the teams have still yet to see their masterpieces up close and personal but there are plans to showcase the assembled projects and host an in-person ACAW 2020 event. Stay tuned alumni for the announcement.

Thank you to our ACAW organizers including a special thank you to Mitchell Bring whose encouragement kept the energy alive when it would have been easier to just throw in the towel! Admiration to Andy Brayman and the Matter Factory for never letting up and Andrew Pries who supported the architects every step of the way. Last but certainly not least a thank you to Omar Kahn who delivered another amazing host session and curator of the event.

My sincere gratitude and thanks to all the team members who participated in ACAW 2020.

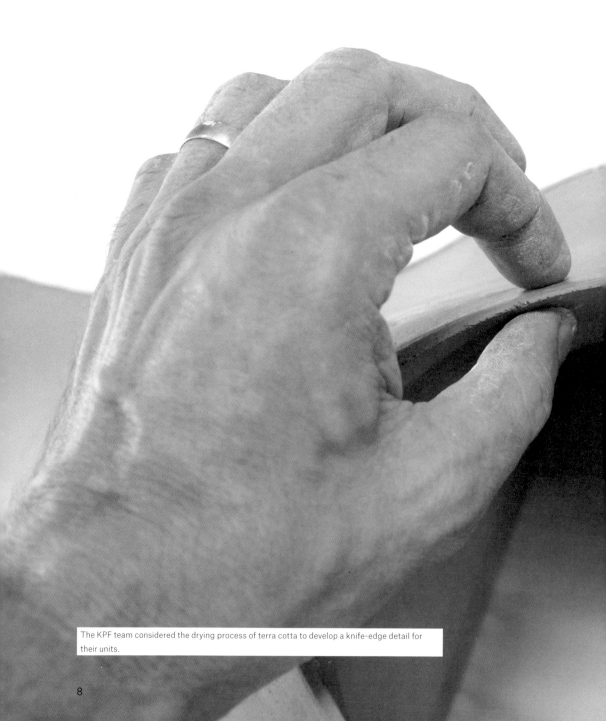

The KPF team considered the drying process of terra cotta to develop a knife-edge detail for their units.

Introduction

Omar Khan

The Alfred University/University at Buffalo team tested the absorption rates in paper molds for their experimental slip-casting project.

The fifth convening of the Architectural Ceramic Assemblies Workshop (ACAW) in 2020, coincided with the onset of the COVID 19 pandemic. The workshop's goal is to educate architects and designers about designing with terracotta. This is done through a consultative process with industry experts at Boston Valley Terra Cotta, who advise the architects to develop their design from schematic to physical prototype. Due to the pandemic, the teams were unable to come together and execute the final step of assembling their custom manufactured ceramic parts. This last step is an important part of the learning experience where all the teams are under one roof working on their assemblies, attending lectures, networking, and discussing the challenges of their projects. It is quite a different thing to lift a terracotta part and align it with a self-similar one than to move a geometrical representation of it on a screen. Weight, texture, color, and warmth of the material became viscerally present and provide important feedback to the designer. Despite this shortcoming, we were able to complete all the prototype assemblies, some with teams coming to the Boston Valley factory to build them individually and others assembled by Boston Valley personnel. While the collective experience of physically coming together was lost this year, a virtual reality gallery was constructed in its place where all the research was collected and could be viewed. This gave some recognition of a collective research investigation despite our isolation. This book builds on that gallery construction to provide a more cross research perspective- themes and concerns- that emerged during this workshop.

The following chapters chronicle the work of the invited architecture teams that included SOM, Pelli Clarke & Partners with Studios Architecture, Kohn Pedersen Fox, LMN Architects, Adrian Smith + Gordon Gill Architecture, Handel Architects, PLP Architecture with Studio Christine Jetten and academic teams Haptek Lab and the University at Buffalo with Alfred University. Some of the teams were assisted on their designs by ACAW sponsor Walter P Moore.

The work is divided into two sections, Surface and Screen. Surface focuses on design research into enclosure systems for architectural surfaces and structures. Terracotta's formal, ornamental and material properties are explored to develop complex geometries, undulating and dynamic parts that seem to freeze in motion, and highly articulated surface effects. The SOM team enclosed a column using terracotta extrusions that were CNC wire cut to expose their interior

LMN team assembles their units.

webbing. These are arrayed around the column creating a rotating dynamic surface for an otherwise conventional structural element. Likewise, Pelli Clarke & Partners with Studios Architecture, developed a fin extrusion that waves in elevation. It's turquoise glaze breaks on its striated edges accentuating its formal qualities. Kohn Pedersen Fox looked to develop an interior surface that seamlessly goes from wall to ceiling, integrating plants, lighting, and other systems into it. The richness of the surface alludes to the highly ornamented surfaces of architecture past without the burdens of historical references. And finally, the work of Haptek Lab utilizes robotic technologies to work the surface of terracotta panels. They reference the pictorial murals of architecture past, which the robotic arms equipped with rollers and stipplers can emulate by precisely marking the terracotta's surface.

Alternatively, Screen focuses on research into more open constructions where terracotta is used to frames apertures, creates cavities for other things to occupy it, tiles that physically move or become a framework that allows for light and air to move through them. These projects explore different manufacturing techniques from extrusions to slip casts, and unique glazes that accentuate the unconventional forms that the designers produced. LMN developed a hexagonal vessel that can aggregate into a Voronoi pattern which allows occupancy by flora and fauna. The freestanding wall emulates something that might be observed in nature from its formal organization to its color variegation. Adrian Smith + Gordon Gill Architecture developed a curvaceous façade frame that integrated glazing and lighting systems. Inspired by Guastavino tiling, the system is envisioned for very tall buildings where its continuous flow would be visually stunning. Handel Architects designed a cable supported fish scale screen that could drape itself on a structure. The scales float upon each other to allow air and light to pass through them but protect against water. PLP Architecture with Studio Christine Jetten explored metallic glazing on slightly wavy tiles that could move on the façade changing the perception of the surface. These explored the added dimension that glaze can bring to the architectural surface which is unique to ceramics. Finally, the team from The University at Buffalo and Alfred University explored developing a rapid prototyping technique that combines cardboard molds and glazes to develop complex sculptural frameworks. Their interest in exploring new and experimental workflows for ceramic design combined digital and craft making techniques.

While each research is unique to the individual team, there are themes that run across the different explorations. These include concerns with sustainability and a more ethical use of materials. Terracotta's low embodied energy, recyclability and ubiquity comes up across the projects. The material's formal and performative properties are the drivers of many projects as well. The ability to be shaped and sculpted, but also its thermal properties factor in much of the research. Additionally, surface effects like texturing and glazing are unique to ceramics and different projects explore variegation and ornamentation in new ways. These explorations seek bioclimatic effects- how the architectural surface interacts with light, air, insolation, water, flora and fauna- to not only optimize building performance but to enhance it and make it playful and visually engaging. Finally, there are explorations of manufacturing techniques and how they can become part of the formal explorations of the design. This is vital goal of the workshop to involve the manufacturer in the design process rather than simply its execution. The experimental use of robotic technologies and imagining the full workflow from design to manufacturing provides a glimpse into the future of architectural ceramics.

Detail of glaze breaking on Pelli Clarke & Partners' and Studios Architecture's striated units

Initial study by Haptek Lab of terra cotta surface patterning by robotic arm.

PLP Architecture with Christine Jetten Studio demonstrate how glaze can augment a tile's formal properties.

Pelli Clarke & Partners' and Studios Architecture's Dynamic Terracotta II

Surface

Post-Extrusion Manipulation of Terra Cotta Profiles

Skidmore, Owings & Merrill

Project team

SOM New York	Amy Garlock, AIA *(Team coordiantor)* *Associate*
SOM Chicago	Eric Pasche, AIA *Associate* Rami Abou-Khalil, RAIC, LEED AP *Associate*

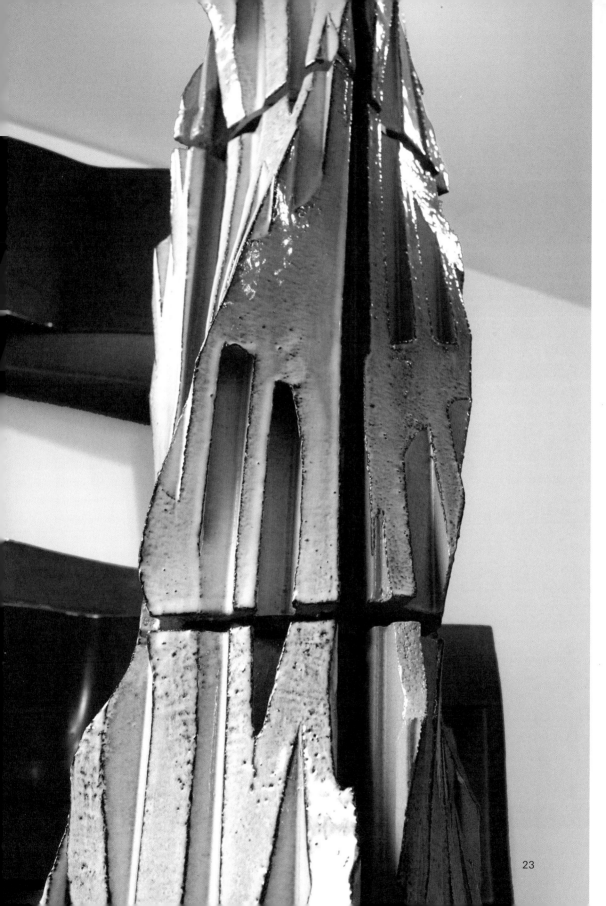

Terra cotta has long been valued for its plasticity and has recently regained popularity in contemporary buildings as architects aim to incorporate historically contextual materials in innovative ways through ornamental patterning. While various methods of carving and casting can be implemented to create almost any shape in terra cotta, as evidenced by the elaborate detailing of many historical references, these methods are often time- and labor-intensive. This makes them ill-suited to most contemporary construction budgets and schedules, leading architects interested in using terra cotta to rely on the largely automated extrusion process which allows faster and more consistent production and lends itself well to the rain screen façade systems being implemented on large projects.

With the added economy of extruded terra cotta also come constraints that must be considered in the design. First, while the range of custom extrusion profiles available gives architects significant design flexibility when it comes to cross-sectional shape, the process inherently creates a rigid reading along the direction of extrusion. Second, the amortized tooling cost of extrusion dies, particularly in the production of smaller runs required for creating variety, can limit the number of unique profiles used on a project and therefore the amount of variability that can be achieved in the design. Finally, attempts to produce continuity between distinct profiles is not supported by this method.

The wire cut panels are threaded through rods and held in place by top and bottom spacers.

In the second year of our research inquiry, team SOM sought to challenge these constraints through post-extrusion manipulation of green terra cotta components. Our 2019 exploration of the possibilities of 5-axis saw cutting showed the ornamental possibilities that carving away from an extrusion can reveal: the hollow internal cells, which are required to create structurally efficient panels and facilitate the drying process; and cut surfaces, which expose the components that make up the clay body. However, it was time- and energy-intensive to cut through terracotta in its fired state, raising questions about whether such a strategy would be appropriate for application across a full façade.

During the 2019 workshop, we also experimented with Boston Valley's 4-axis wire cutter to carve unfired extrusions. The wire cutter offers two distinct advantages over saw cutting methods: because it is used to manipulate terracotta in its unfired state, it is faster and less energy intensive than cuts made after firing. Furthermore, since the wire is set on a rotating ring, through which the soft clay passes as it is pushed on a conveyor belt, the wire cutter also allows an expanded range of forming options, as it can be used to create both straight cuts and ruled-surface cuts. We began our 2020 exploration with this tool as our premise and worked with the team at Boston Valley to design an assembly that would showcase the potential to use the wire cutter to manipulate extruded terracotta.

The multi layered glaze is designed to highlight the web pattern.

We tested various extrusion profiles on the wire cutter in early experimentation with the Boston Valley team, using standard dies to understand the ways in which the machine could (or could not) cut various geometric profiles. These experiments taught us a few lessons: first, that the wire cutter was best suited to cutting sweeping ruled-surface geometries, rather than geometries with sharp changes in direction. Directional changes in the cut often led to dragging of the extruded piece along the conveyor feed, or deviations from the intended cut plane. Second, we learned that more interesting results came from die shapes with gridded and denser internal cellular structures. Since there were more cell walls to cut through, the resultant cut pieces were more intricate and revealed unexpected patterns.

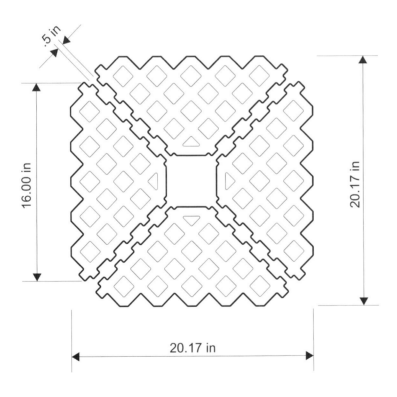

The extruded profile is arrayed around a central void; these arrayed waffle grids represent the extrusions prior to the cutting of each piece by the CAD-driven wire-cutter.

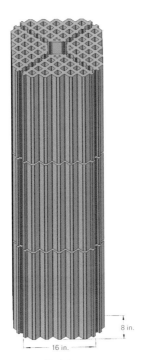

8 in.

16 in.

Fired size

Cutting surfaces

Cut geometry

Cut geometry

Discrete piece cut geometry
all types

Cut geometry options were tested in a 3d digital model to simulate the cutting planes of the wire cutter. Single ruled surfaces were made possible by the four-axis wire-cutter, producing a dynamic column geometry.

Finally, we learned that there was a textural contrast between the smooth surface of the extruded piece and the wire-struck surface of the cut plane as the grog in the clay responded to the wire. We decided to embrace this new grain by working with ceramic artist Andy Brayman to formulate a glaze application strategy that would enhance the contrast between the wire-struck surface and the smooth extruded surfaces. A dark blue engobe glaze was applied to the cut surface with a paint roller and allowed to dry. The whole piece was then sprayed with a white over-glaze. When fired, the blue glaze showed through the over-glaze and further defined the cut surfaces through color.

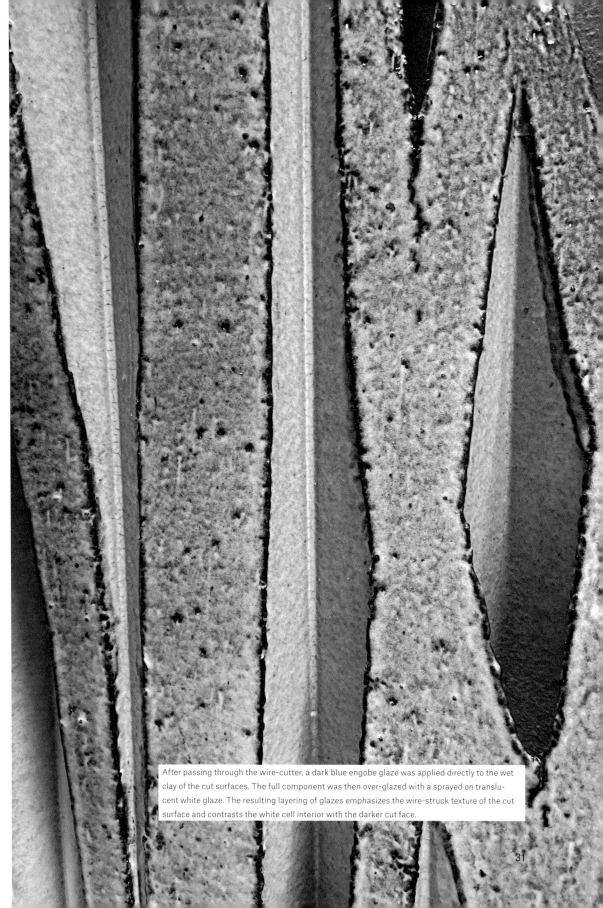

After passing through the wire-cutter, a dark blue engobe glaze was applied directly to the wet clay of the cut surfaces. The full component was then over-glazed with a sprayed on translucent white glaze. The resulting layering of glazes emphasizes the wire-struck texture of the cut surface and contrasts the white cell interior with the darker cut face.

For the final prototype, we worked with the Boston Valley team to design an extrusion die profile in conjunction with the design for an assembly intended to be viewed in the round. The prototype is a clad column, created by stacking the extrusions and cutting through their face and internal webbing with ruled surfaces defined on their edges by four rotated spirals. The die profile is a trapezoidal waffle grid, rotated 45 degrees relative to the base plane with fifteen internal cells separated by 1″ thick walls. We designed the assembly with ½″ separation between pieces to allow for some material tolerance and for support structure. In the final design there were three typical pieces, each repeated four times to create a flowing rotationally symmetrical column made up of twelve pieces.

The structural system for the column uses each extruded piece as a gravity support for the piece above. A structural tube at the center holds separator plates, and a threaded rod passes through the voids of the pieces to hold each to the central post. Tightening the rods helps the terracotta self-support in compression.

Inner structure of the 6' tall column prototype assembled at Boston Valley Terracotta in October of 2020.

Our team assembled the column in October 2020. The column support structure was built out from a welded steel base plate and vertical 6″ diameter steel pipe. Half inch plywood spacers hold the pieces apart both vertically and horizontally. Steel threaded rods run through the innermost cell of each of the terracotta pieces and run through slotted holes in the spacer plates. These spacer plates also hold each level of the column together. When the topmost pieces are added, the nut at the top of each threaded rod is tightened to hold the assembly together through compression. The assembly brought to light a few tolerance issues with both the material itself and the means of manipulation. In some cases, there were up to ½″ deviations in length between fired pieces, which we can attribute to material behavior both as it was cut and as it dried.

Despite these discrepancies, the component parts flow together almost seamlessly to create a sculptural fluted column with a contemporary twist demonstrating the forming and alignment potential of post-extrusion component manipulation by the CNC wire cutter. The loose early experimentation has led to unexpected formal languages in the final terracotta form that will continue to inform our future projects. A careful understanding of material tolerances could be built up with more experimentation with this new machine. We think that this knowledge coupled with calibration of the cut surface profile through parametric design and study of more complex geometric possibilities would be a productive next step for research of wire cutter applications toward more economical mass customization.

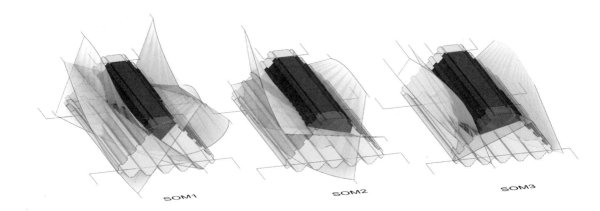

Diagrams illustrate the three ruled surfaces that were used to cut each of the extruded pieces. The sequencing of these cuts required iterative testing with the SOM team and the team operating the wire cutter at Boston Valley's plant.

Detail of the prototype assembly in progress.

An imagined array of taller wire-cut columns in a virtual gallery space, shared for the virtual ACAW presentation in August 2020.

Initial assembly of the 6-foot tall prototype column at Boston Valley Terracotta, October 2020

Extruded, wire-cut and glazed pieces being prepared for assembly at Boston Valley Terra Cotta.

Dynamic Terra Cotta II

Pelli Clarke & Partners, Studios Architecture, Walter P Moore

Project team

Pelli Clarke Pelli Architects	Craig Copeland
	Principal, AIA LEED AP BD+C
	Kristin Hopkins-Clegg
	Associate Principal
	Pedja Bilinac
	Senior Associate
	Brad Loew
	Designer
	Zhe Huang
	Designer
Studios Architecture	Graham Clegg
	Principal
	Zach Bark
	Associate
	Brian Kim
	Associate
Walter P Moore	Erik Verboon
	Principal, Managing Director NY Office,
	Director of Enclosure Engineering

41

Our team had the opportunity to pursue research we started in ACAW 2019 to further understand the nuances of the material. Although our initial research focused on innovative tooling to facilitate the automated production of varied forms from simple terra cotta extrusion, this year our team was interested in working through the affordances and challenges of the material that were revealed from our initial prototypes. Through hands-on experience and informed by the deep knowledge of the Boston Valley team of experts, we worked on controlling the stress imposed by the formal manipulation on the material, how the component parts would align with one another, and also the perception of the assembly by the viewer.

We began research in ACAW 2020 by digging deeper to resolve two key aspects of the fabrication constraints our design imposed on our previous prototype. The first focus was on creating a reliable method for mass-producing terra cotta extrusions that could be variably modified in the wet state, and would still fire into true, properly squared panels. This involved changes to both the fabrication and the form of our units. The second was to develop shapes and glazing that would highlight form through color and surface vitrification which we did not have an opportunity to explore the previous year.

By design, the 2019 extrusion was asymmetrical: an L shape resulting from combining a conventional, flat panel rainscreen with a projected fin. The combination was to provide basic effectiveness of the repeating, standard rectangular panel along with tunable expressions from the projections. The intention being to build upon a proven industrial-scaled cladding method—the rectangular rainscreen—with the integration of a fin that a robotic arm might shape along a conveyor, between the extrusion and firing states. For these experimental units, we imposed a wave on the fin through manual manipulation. The robotic arm movements would be directed by a parametric-planned array, resulting in cost-effective, industrial-scaled approach to custom-made rainscreens.

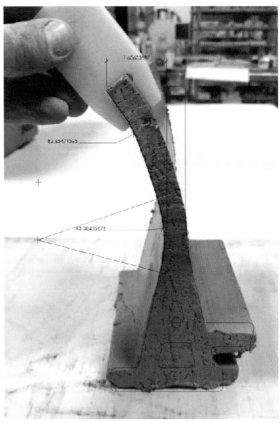

The robotic finger mock-up bends the extruded terracotta fin in its wet state (left). The 2019 assembly shows the unplanned warping of the fins wile firing due to their asymmetric form (right).

There were two problems with our prototype in 2019 which we set out to address in 2020. First, the asymmetrical extrusions heated unevenly, causing the otherwise rectangular panels to warp and the fins to crack undesirably under the stress; second, we were not able to find an effective method for the robotic arm to shape the fin. In consultation with Boston Valley Terra Cotta we were able to successfully address the stress problem and continue to work on the digitally controlled manipulation.

We took our 2019 extruded form, mirrored it, and included a sacrificial bridge between the two. The idea was proposed by John Krouse, CEO of Boston Valley, as a corrective to warping and stress-fracturing of our 2019 extrusions. The Krouse proposal of firing the mirrored extrusion, a double-L shape, was successful. The connecting bridge in the middle was easily cut out to release two L shape panels. Furthermore, even with the fins bent in different (non-mirroring) configurations, there was no warping.

We manipulated the fin manually following a set of forms that gave more control to the deformation. Unfortunately, as with the 2019 research, we were not able to resolve the robotic bending intervention. To not hinder other aspects of the research, Peter Schmidt of Boston Valley, created Styrofoam jigs for hand-bending the fins before firing.

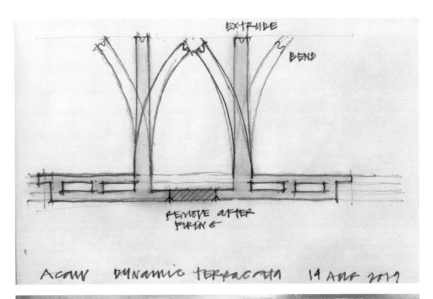

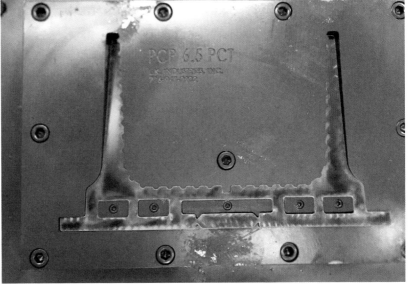

The modification of the 2019 extruded form was sketched to show how it is mirrored to minimize uneven firing. Based on this diagram Boston Valley produced the extrusion plate for the final 2020 design.

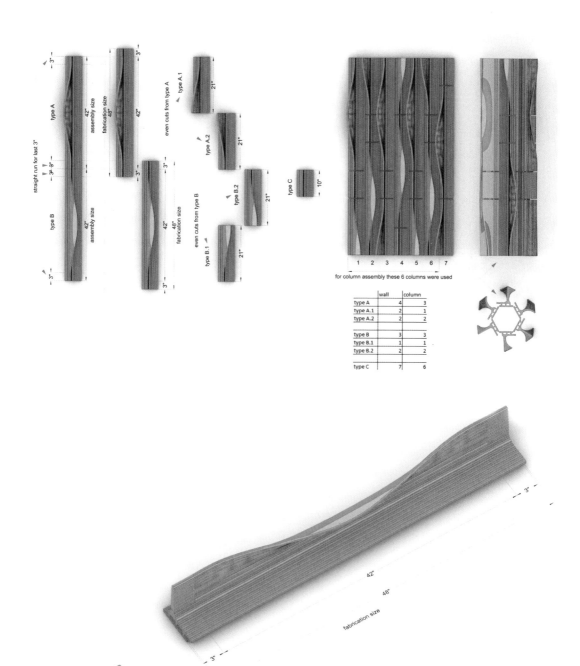

straight run for last 3"

type A
42" assembly size
48" fabrication size
3" 3" 3"

even cuts from type A

type A.1 21"
type A.2 21"

type B
42" assembly size
3"

42" 48" fabrication size
3"

even cuts from type B

type B.1 21"
type B.2 21"

type C 10"

for column assembly these 6 columns were used
1 2 3 4 5 6 7

	wall	column
type A	4	3
type A.1	2	1
type A.2	2	2
type B	3	3
type B.1	1	1
type B.2	2	2
type C	7	6

42"
48" fabrication size
3"
3"

Kit-of-parts layouts and the inventory of wall and column assemblies (above) are used to guide work during the ACAW workshop.

The team next focused on addressing the continuity of the pattern through the aggregated panels. The continuous flow was dependent on precise alignment of the ends of the fins. To facilitate this, we established all panels to end with their fins at 90-degrees to their backing. We observed that this was compromised in the first iteration of the system by the relation of the wave part of the fin to its end. Providing a greater distance from the waves to the ends to allow each fin to maintain its form in the drying and firing process. To increase variation, we occasionally included shorter and straight (unbent) sections. This way we were able to explore multiple assembly options. We ultimately chose to build two variations for the same kit of parts: flat (a surface) and in the round (a column).

Virtual 3D studies of the fin texturing and color and the full-length panel with its controlled bend helped define the final unit form and texture.

The team was interested in adding another layer to our understanding of architectural terracotta by exploring how surface texturing and glazing could affect the visual expression of the form. We were intent on producing amplified readings of the curving surfaces by manipulating color and shadow. Following the suggestion of Andy Brayman of the Matter Factory, a ceramic and glazing consultant at ACAW, we studied a variety of repeating grooves in tandem with different glazing recipes.

The intent was twofold; to create opportunities for the glaze to pool across the panel face resulting in a rich range of color tones, and utilize a glaze with a rich chromatic range that worked well on both a smooth or textured surface. After trying ranges of blues, purples and browns through both digital models and fired samples, we ultimately chose to use Brayman's recipe for aqua/blue green. The effect resonated with us in part because of the positive associations to a richly patinated copper. But it had an added benefit of material resilience and of vitrified color in varying depths. To heighten the effect, we designed a linear texturing for the insides of the double-L's and left the outsides smooth. Furthermore, we designed the texture to maintain a flat surface on the groove tops to help limit pinch marks on the peaks when the fins went through the bending process.

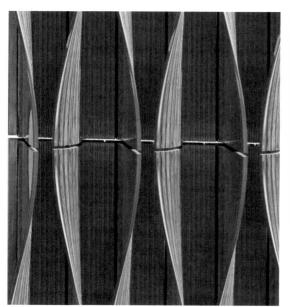 

Glazing, color and texture on varying clay bodies, and glaze flow studies were done on curved surfaces.

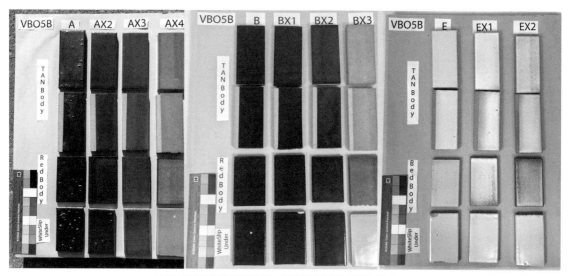

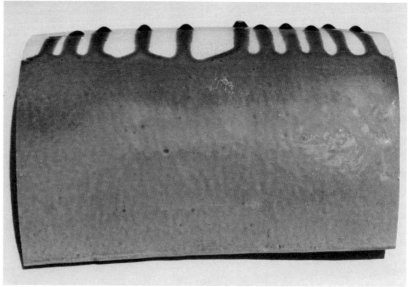

Glaze tests were also done to understand the affect of the linear patten on color.

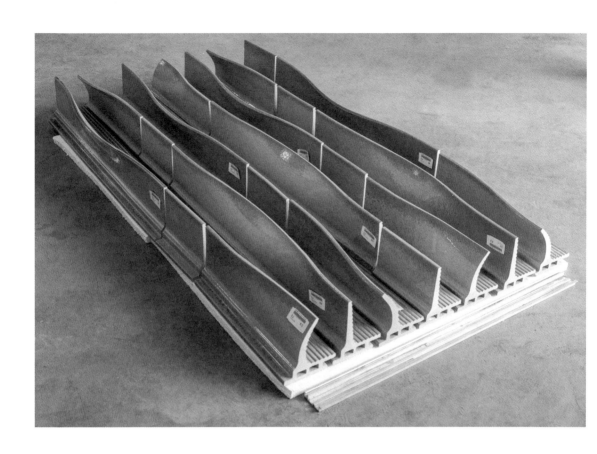

Dry-lay of rain-screen assembly prior to workshop assembly (above). Column assembly in progress (right).

We made great progress with the 2020 research, but still the possibility of robotic manipulation is underexplored. We speculate that as interest in terra cotta facades grows in larger commercial applications, due to their need for distinct patterning, robotic arm forming may prove a productive technology to explore.

Final assemblies at the 2020 ACAW Workshop of a wall rain-screen and column.

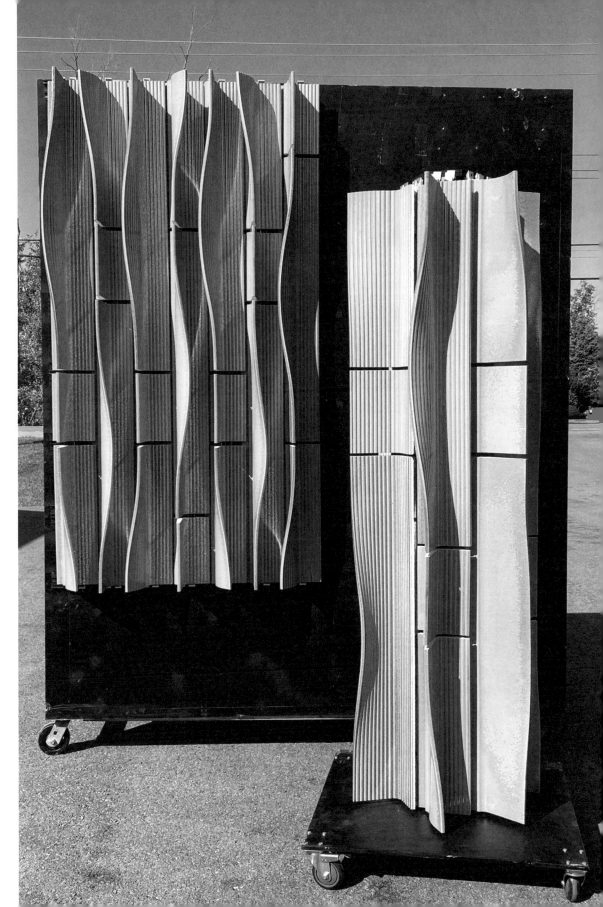

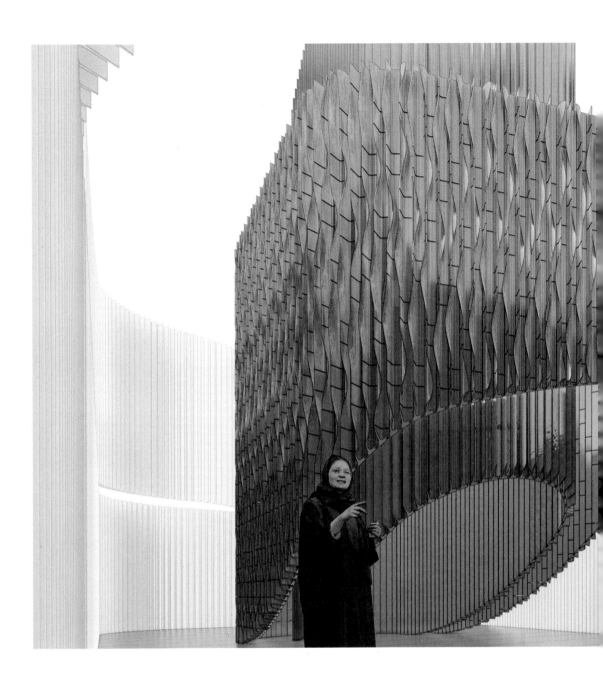

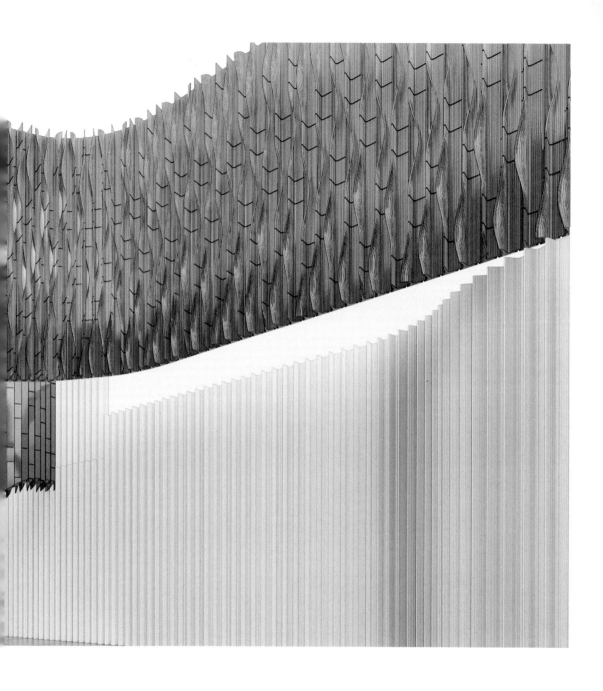

Our epilogue to this research chapter is a virtual room we designed showcasing the potential expansion of our assembly, elevating architectural place with dynamic terracotta.

Locating the "Green" in the "Wall"

Kohn Pedersen Fox

Project team

Kohn Pedersen Fox	Darina Zlateva *(Team coordinator)*
	Senior Associate Principal
	Marianne Kwok
	Design Director
	Chuqi Liu
	Architectural Designer
	Asli Oney
	Digital Fabrication Manager
Ceramic Artist	Andy Brayman
Walter P Moore	Gustav Fagerstron
	Principal

For ACAW 2020's workshop and virtual exhibition, KPF advanced a pursuit for sustainable materials and assemblies in the development of an interior "Green Wall". The use of the term "green" refers to both plant life in the wall as well as building materials that are environmentally responsible because they are composed of renewables and take steps to reduce the embodied carbon of the assembly. This led the team to research material lifecycles and sustainable sourcing. Coupling terra cotta's low carbon footprint with a glaze composed of post-industrial recycled glass created a compelling proposal for a new sustainable development in downtown Vancouver. Meanwhile, the formal development of the units and their aggregation uses the plasticity of the ceramic material to respond to specific functional requirements that wall/ceiling assemblies often fail to integrate well. The prototype considers the "green" or sustainable aspects of the assembly in parallel with the biophilic expression of an ornamental "green wall" locating the green within its material makeup, form, and organization.

Designing a sustainable lobby wall started with a rigorous examination of embodied carbon in building materials. We looked at the Building Materials Pyramid, first created by CINARK. This pyramid can be thought of as the complement to the food pyramid; your plate should be mostly veggies (timber) and spare on meat (metals). The pyramid charts Embodied Carbon ($kgCO_2e/kg$). While local stone is relatively low in embodied carbon (0.50 for slate), clients have a strong preference for super white stones with minimal veining found in very few places on Earth. Practically speaking, this makes natural stones for "Class A" lobbies have a much higher embodied carbon, estimated at 1.10 $kgCO_2e/kg$, making them more akin to structural steel (1.13 $kgCO_2e/kg$) or linoleum (1.10 $kgCO_2e/kg$).

Representation of a full wall assembly (above). The terracotta prototype partially de-molded.

The prototype was created with a RAM press. A blue foam model of the design was used to create a lower and upper mold which formed the terra cotta piece.

Closeup of de-molding the piece from the upper and lower mold.

Meanwhile, unglazed terra cotta has a relatively low embodied carbon at 0.40 kg CO_2e/kg. The issue becomes sourcing the frit (the mixture of silica and fluxes which is fused at high temperature to make glass) required to create a glass glaze (glaze is how you create color and gloss on a terra cotta tile). This frit is inevitably globally sourced and thus increases the embodied carbon of the material. With this in mind, Andy Brayman began experimenting with post-industrial glass to create a sustainable, but stable, glaze for production. The KPF glaze was developed to melt sufficiently by using 100 percent Type 1 Recycled Borosilicate glass in lieu of traditional commercial frits that use only pure minerals direct from the mining industry. The Recycled Borosilicate glass is a post-industrial product that is sourced domestically, which helps to keep it out of the landfill. In this way, Andy was able to cut down embodied carbon by 50 percent, down to an estimated 0.67 kgCO_2e/kg.

In addition to its sustainable qualities, terra cotta is celebrated for its versatility: it can be formed into complex shapes and glazed into an infinite set of colors and finishes. For the form of the lobby feature, we wanted to use bulbous, curved shapes to achieve a seamless transition from vertical wall to horizontal ceiling. We designed a nested panel system that would hold plants close to the ground where people would come into contact with them, enhancing biophilic attributes. It transforms as it reaches the ceiling to accommodate other functions. Typically, the lobby ceiling presents a distinct challenge as it requires hosting a long list of practical elements such as lights, sprinklers, signage, speakers, diffusers, wifi boxes, fire alarm speaker strobes, cameras, sensors, and many more. To achieve the seamless look, we designed a set of apertures in the terra cotta panels that would accommodate this variety of ceiling elements.

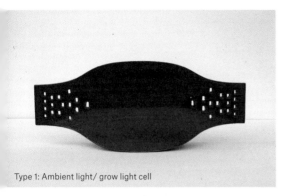

Type 1: Ambient light/ grow light cell

Type 2: Ceiling aperture cell

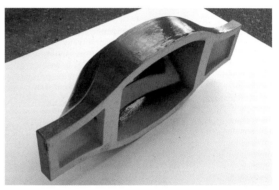

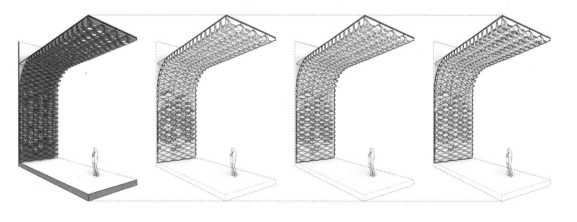

1. Integrated wall to
   ceiling system

2. Plants

3. Grow lights
   and ambient lights

4. Ceiling elements:
   sprinklers, speakers,
   diffusers,lights, etc.

The design intent was to achieve a seamless transition from vertical wall to horizontal ceiling. The nested panel system of "cells" hosts the various features and elements that are required in a lobby (plants, lights, diffusers, sprinklers, etc.).

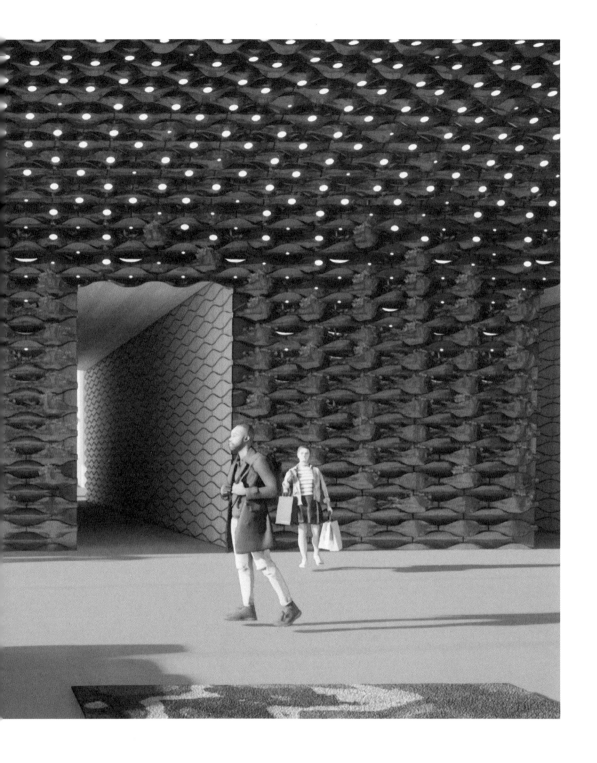

Visualizations of the lobby wall explored the placement of planter units in the system.

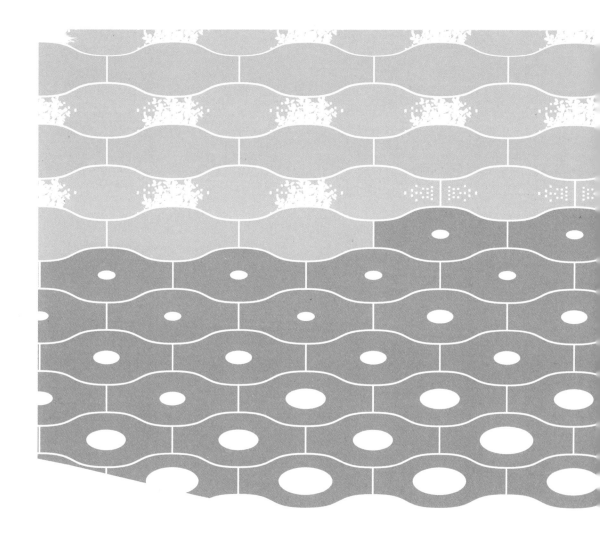

The three cell types were:

> — Aperture Cells: The large openings allowed digital screens behind the terra cotta to add to the ambiance of the lobby. The addition of digital screens was a client request—they expected a lot of their future tenants to be technology-focused and wanted the ability to celebrate their work in the main lobby. Smaller openings would be used for the practical elements such as sprinklers and speakers.
>
> — Glazing Windows: The subtle design inspired by Andy Brayman's artwork creates a thinned-out glaze pocket through which light travels. These micro apertures were an opportunity to add grow lights or down lighting for the plants.
>
> — Planting beds: The cupped-out cells were sized for enough soil to sponsor a grouping of living plants.

type 1   type 2   type 3

The diagram presents the three unit types, how the cuts are altered in the blue units, and how they aggregated.

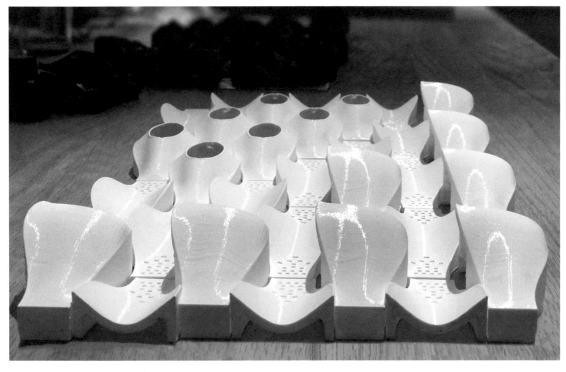

3D printed units were used to test the pattern combination and fit between components.

Before glazing, we 3D-printed the shapes 1-to-1 in the KPF Maker Space to test the light and shadow of the various curved profiles, to micro-adjust the fit between panels, and to test pattern combinations in the aggregation of panels. We looked at quarter inch tolerances between cells to ensure they would operate correctly (ex: that the cell behind a plant cell would be flat enough to provide space for the plants to grow). Cells were designed one inch thick, but minimal in weight by the addition of voids in the cells. To ease de-molding, we added rounded edges with a 3 percent inclination to each face.

For the color, we selected a gradient between greens and blues to enhance the experience of the wall and mapped the color by use. We wanted the plant cells to be green to reinforce the liveliness of the flora on the wall. Secondarily, should a plant need replanting, the green terra cotta would maintain that green pixel in the overall wall composition. The ceiling aperture cells were blue. This mapping recalled the sky, but practically, the darker blue minimized glare for the digital screens and was complementary to the blue light emitted by most digital screens. The result was a vibrant forest landscape of glossy terra cotta.

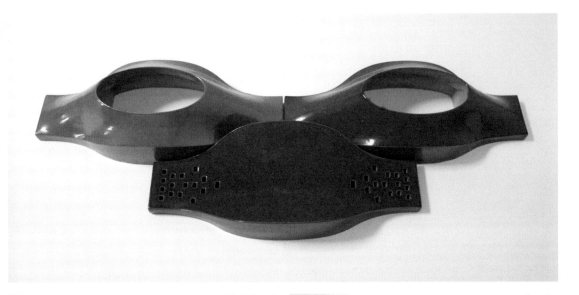

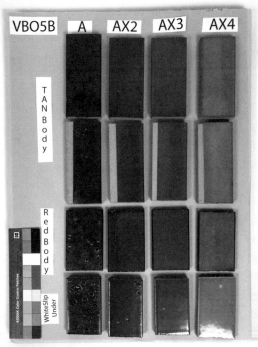

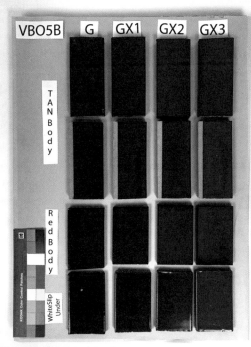

Color tests created by Andy Brayman using the recycled post-industrial glass glaze he developed. In the final design, green was mapped to plant cells, blue to ceiling aperture cells and a gradient was selected for the in between cells.

The wall assembly of the terra cotta units was designed by Gustav Fagerstrom of Walter P. Moore. Using a Keil anchor, the terra cotta units would be attached to horizontal rails which would in turn attach to vertical z-girts. The transition from vertical to horizontal at the corner of wall and ceiling would be achieved with short substructure spans, the closer spaced, the smoother the curve. The pattern lends itself nicely to unitization for large swaths of flat horizontal and vertical units, thus bringing economy and ease of construction.

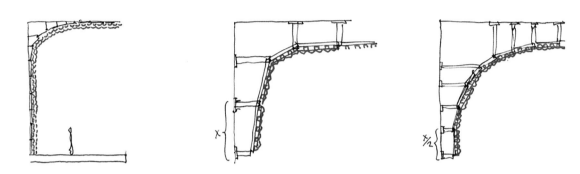

Wall-to-ceiling transition: shorter substructure spans → smoother curve.

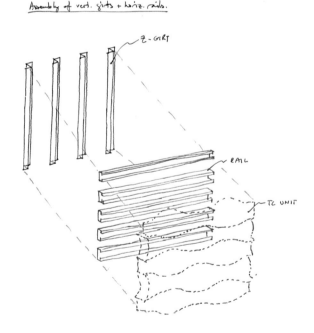

Gustav Fagerstrom sketches of the Kiel anchor system allowing unitized panels to be mounted along a curve.

The unitized panels are hung along a structural curve that transitions from from wall to ceiling.
The structural fins are embedded in the wall but emerge as the system transitions to the ceiling.

The digital space of the 2020 ACAW exhibition allowed us to re-imagine the elements of the lobby into a simulation of clouds over a green terra cotta forest. For this virtual installation, we create an immersive tunnel that can be experienced through our animation path designed for an eye level experience of walking through the space. We positioned plant cells at the entry to highlight the "green" aspects of the project. We wanted to play up the light and shadow of the undulating terra cotta profiles, so we pulled the transformation from convex to concave across the length of the tunnel. On the digital screens up above, we mapped slowly color changing animations of clouds. On playing the video, we were struck by how layered the space felt. Once built, it would be amplified with smells, sounds and visuals—a green wall becoming a sensual landscape.

A still from the final video depicting the immersive and sensory experience of walking through the Nanogon display tunnel.

Beyond the Surface: Haptics in Robotic Craft

Haptek Lab

Project team

Ryerson University School of Interior Design	**Linda Zhang** (*Team coordinator*) *Assistant Professor* **Jonathon Anderson** *Associate Professor and Director, Design +* *Technology Lab at The Creative School* **Georgia Barrington** *Research Assistant* **Amy Yan** *Research Assistant* **Reese Young** *Research Assistant*
Syracuse University School of Art, Ceramics	**Errol Willett** *Associate Professor*
Cal Poly San Luis Obispo, Architecture Department	**Clare Olsen** *Professor*
Cornell University, AAP, Department of Architecture	**Naomi Frangos** *Visiting Associate Professor*

The project involved studying the qualities of the clay that resulted from working it by hand.

For Haptek Lab, an interdisciplinary team of artists, architects, technologists, interior designers, academics and practitioners, ACAW 2020 provided an opportunity to develop an industrial manufacturing system that integrates craft sensibilities and effects found in ceramic art. This project challenges the disconnect between digital fabrication and the tactile or haptic qualities of material behavior, moving towards a new robotic materiality that operates in the space between machine and artist, robot and operator, industrial and bespoke.

The study began by exploring the tactile qualities of working with clay by hand and using typical techniques such as stamping, molding, and bas relief to create detailed ornamental tiles. Starting with a standard set of clay tools, artists on the team worked intuitively to produce multi-layered, textured surfaces. The team then studied the qualities of these techniques. Indexing manual manipulation of wet clay allowed us to observe the behavior of the terra cotta clay body in response to impressions made by human touch. Given the focus of these studies, the hand manipulations of clay were particularly compelling: fingerprints and depressions, varying slump forms in the wet clay, inexact depths and spacing of maneuvers all created a sense of bodily physicality. Intrigued by these nuances, we set out to translate these qualities using robotic tools.

A custom five-sided 3d printed end-of- arm tool for the KUKA KR10 1100 Agilus robotic arm produced fingerprint-like impressions in the clay.

Due to the clay's hardness and density, as well as the speed of factory settings, we saw the robot as a critical partner when scaling craft sensibilities for industrial fabrication. The robot provides the kind of "strength" required to shape the industrial terra cotta akin to how a human typically shapes artisanal clay that is much less dense and easier to manipulate. However, the robot's strength was so great that it treated the dense material as if it were not there at all– as if it were as light as air. The result was a condition of machine "insensitivity" where the tool had no perception of the force it exerted or the plasticity of the clay. One of our biggest challenges was overcoming this: learning how to program "sensitivity" into the robot's movements.

Testing the translation of craft sensibilities in scale and tooling, our early robotic experiments on Boston Valley Terra Cotta's standard extrusions involved simply attaching a ceramic hand tool to the robotic arm to mimic hand marking. It became obvious there was a lot more to developing the robot's sense of touch than just transferring tools between hand and robot. Our tools were not 'smart' in that they involved no force sensors or feedback data, and therefore required more of a conversation between the Artists on the team and the robot programmers. This conversation was our effort to bridge robot programming with the tactile knowledge of working with clay.

Similar to working with the potter's wheel, the potter needs to first learn to collaborate with the wheel to shape the clay. This type of haptic communication between the potter, the wheel and the clay didn't happen automatically with the robot. Craft needs skill development—how the tool shapes the clay, the deformation it makes, the relationship between speed and effect, all impact how the character of the material communicates. Like the potter's expression, 'slow wheel, soft clay', we needed to first become more attuned to the nuances of the robot's behavior.

To better understand the impacts of the robot's force on the clay, we started by slowing down the robot using manual controls on the teach pendant and documented each action versus speed. As clay deforms its moisture shapes its behavior, it forms ridges, sticks to the tool or peels off. As a result, we quickly realized that our tests were not comparable. However, these findings helped us recognize that this unpredictability was precisely what we were interested in. This led to an exploration of how to program (communicate) sensitivity into the machine through both development of new end-effector tools for the robotic arm and ways to move, sense, and touch the terracotta with those tools. We needed to program haptic sensibility into the tooling process to allow the robot to account for (or in anthropomorphic terms—to sense or feel) the clay's behavior.

A test panel using robotic tooling on a Boston Valley Terracotta panel. By using a five-sided end-of-arm tool, a variety of contrasting marks can be achieved from a single tool.

We returned to the basics with the robot by working slowly and simply making marks using randomized computationally scripted points as we did by hand. This contrasts with conventional uses of robots that harness speed, precision, and accuracy. We treated the digital process just as an artist might, repeating the same action to see what might appear, developing a feedback loop between the textural qualities produced rather than trying to make the clay conform to a premeditated image. We found the more compelling marks to be those suggesting finger-like impressions—textures that were not meant to mimic the hand, but rather to recall the qualities of the hand in a way that would be recognizable and familiar to viewers. In this way, with our robot collaborator, we began building skills over time in "training" ourselves and the robot using programming and tools to elicit the sensual qualities of the resulting material effects.

The team saw an opportunity to work with the robot to develop a new craft vocabulary that would explore what makes the robot unique and surprising: the sub-millimeter precision of robotic tooling, the possibility of infinite variability through digital automation, and the ability to collaborate between machine and human operator and create a feedback loop to generate new and unique products. We used Grasshopper to program a movement pattern informed by an image. Any image can be given as an input parameter as well as any dimension and number of panels to tile the image over. To create a less uniform pattern and imbue the robot with a sensibility of touch, a seed-generated algorithm was used to randomly assign variations in speed and depth to touchpoints. A lexicon of preset and non-repeating patterns verified through the machine-operator feedback loop was assigned across different tones in the image and across the panels to create bespoke patterns.

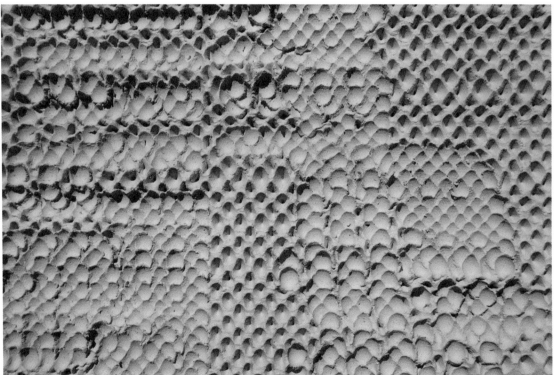

Haptek Lab member Georgia Barrington partnering with the robot on manipulating the clay surface at the Design + Technology Lab at the Creative School, Toronto (above). The resulting terracotta panel after robotic tooling (below).

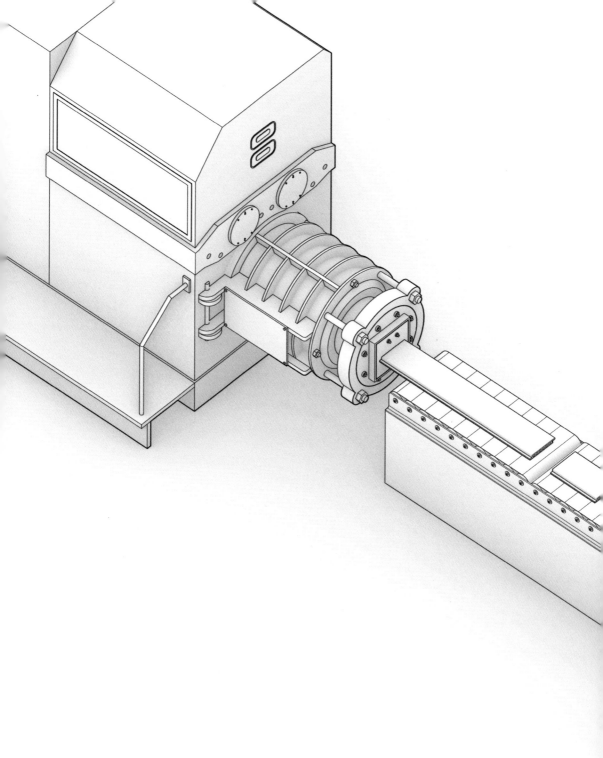

Diagram of integrated robots in manufacturing of architectural ceramics collaborating to create bespoke panels.

In the final stages, we undertook a series of performance optimizations. The robot's six-axis of motion affords up to five different tools on a single industrial robot, seamlessly changing between them. We calibrated relationships amongst impressions made by larger tools with detailing achieved by smaller tools to reduce tooling time and accelerate the process. Optimizing speed becomes an important factor when scaling craft to industrial manufacturing processes. Human speeds of marking and making found in a typical potter studio simply cannot keep up with the speed of industrial manufacturing. However, moving at 3.2 meters per second, our Kuka robotic arm became a critical collaborator allowing robotic touch to keep up with the speed of industrial production. In an industrial setting, multiple robots could also work side by side to produce an endless variety of images, patterns, and textures. Through careful design of end effectors and operations, our team was able to create high-density textures at industrial speeds that maintained our craft goals.

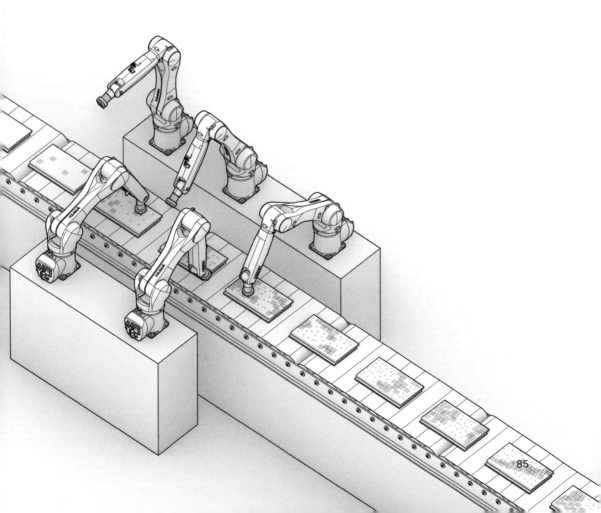

Our process integrates a new kind of robotic craft and potential innovation in architectural ceramics. Operating at speeds in concert with production at sub-millimeter accuracy and repeatability, it also makes otherwise highly laborious surface detailing and finishing more accessible for mass production. Through programmed sensitivity, the robot is calibrated to produce tactile qualities and a more sensual experience of machined clay. We envision this process unlocking new possibilities for the experience of industrially produced ceramics.

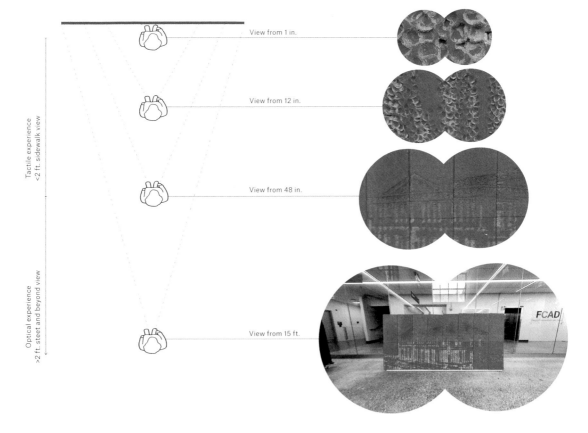

Study of the haptic experiences of the robotically-tooled clay surface from various distances.

For the virtual ACAW 2020, we aimed to produce an image to be experienced in motion relative to its viewers. In the Haptek Lab VR exhibition, we move towards the image on the 1:1 scale mockup, the figure begins to fade as its tactile qualities become more vivid. In the next phase of this project, Haptek Lab aims to further develop this aspect, exploring how designs translate across scales from the tactile to the scenographic.

We would like to acknowledge funding support from Ryerson University and Syracuse University as well as in-kind contributions from the Creative Technology Lab at FCAD, Boston Valley Terracotta, the Ryerson RSID 3D Material Studio and Ceramic Lab, Ryerson Collaboratory, Corning Museum of Glass, the Syracuse University Ceramics Department and Cal Poly San Luis Obispo College of Architecture and Environmental Design.

Detail of alternative tile stippling pattern.

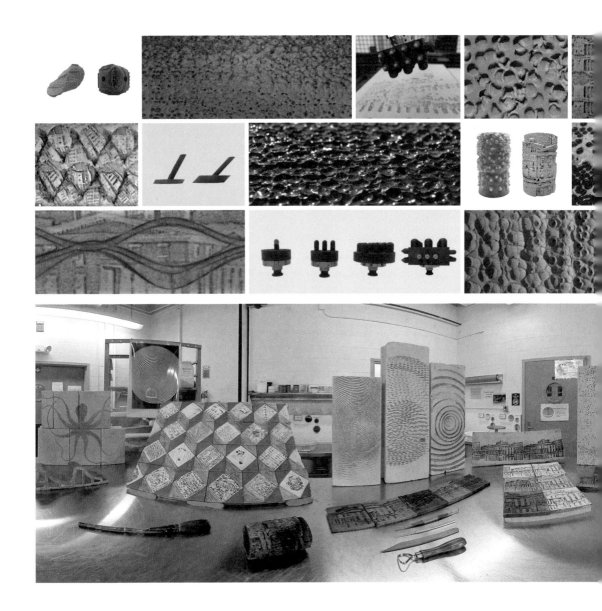

Virtual reality gallery of various custom 3D printed end-of-arm tools as well as their resulting impressions on the terracotta panels (above). A panoramic photograph of experimental test panels in the Syracuse University Ceramic Department glaze lab, Syracuse, NY (below).

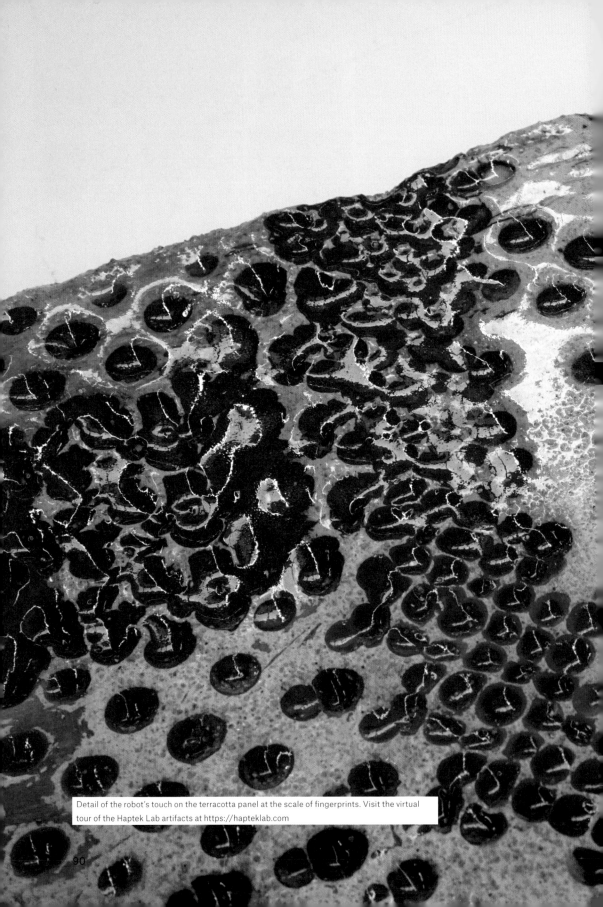

Detail of the robot's touch on the terracotta panel at the scale of fingerprints. Visit the virtual tour of the Haptek Lab artifacts at https://hapteklab.com

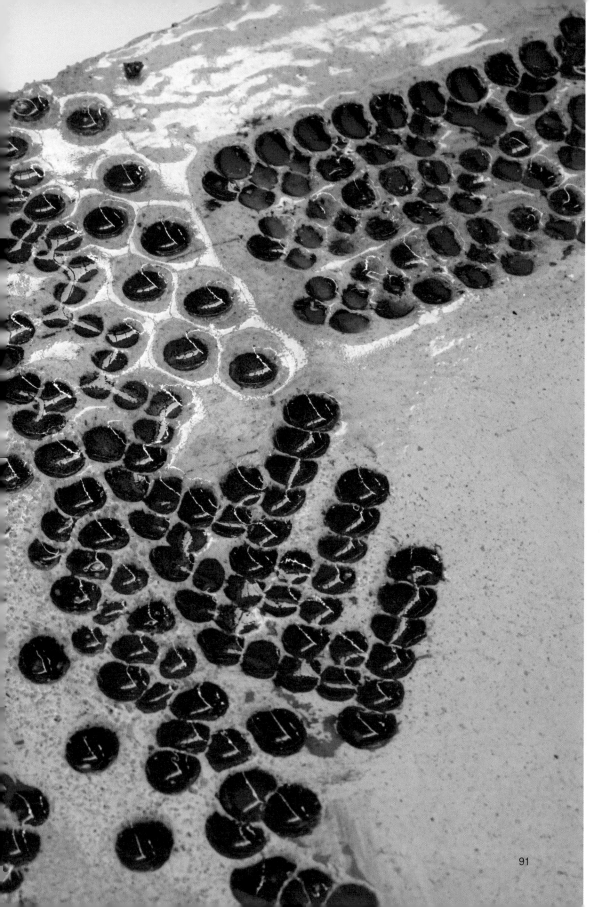

Dynamic Masonry

PLP Architecture and Studio Christine Jetten

Project team

PLP Architecture	Daniel Moore *(Team coordinator)*
	Partner
	Wayne McKiernan
	Partner
	Andrew Crombie
	Senior Associate
	Yijun Huang
	Architect
Studio Christine Jetten	Christine Jetten
	Founder
Arup	Alexis Harrison
	Associate

PLP Architecture has worked on several masonry buildings with brick and terracotta facades around the world. It's one of our favorite materials—and we like to use it as a covering that gets applied, sometimes universally and sometimes in select areas, to a project in a manner that instills it with a sense of solidity, strength, and beauty.

We had always wanted to explore additional ways that this material could be utilized to achieve a lighter and more dynamic effect that possessed an inherent kinetic energy. When Christine Jetten, the renowned ceramicist with whom we had worked in the early 2000s, joined our design teams for two recent projects in Central London, we began to think about ways we might explore pushing this forward—looking at how we could take best advantage of the very special glazes that she could design and engineer.

We felt that, as a starting point, adapting the registration of light and reflectivity upon the glaze could bring particularly special results. We liked the idea of altering the fluidity of this light through the movement of terracotta elements, achieved perhaps through their faceting in a manner not unlike a cut diamond or even a disco ball. Looking back on our past experiences, we decided that a dark and reflective glaze would be useful, as this could provide a strong contrast between faces that reflect light and those which do not.

We also wanted to find the means to allow the tiles to move to produce a more dynamic sculptural composition that could take advantage of the qualities present in the glazing. We looked to buildings that could serve as precedents for this: The Debenhams Department Store on Oxford Street, London interested us, with its metallic veil that shimmers in the breeze like water on a lake. Similarly, The Institut du Monde Arabe, Paris actively adjusts to permit constantly changing light into the building's interior depending on the sun's position and intensity.

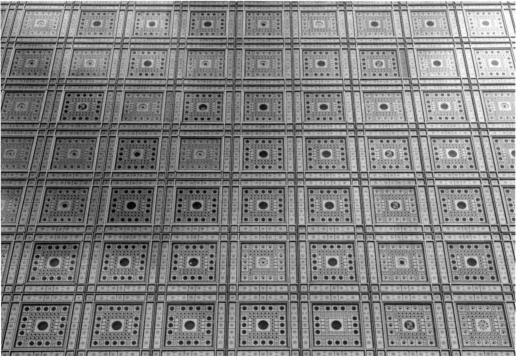

Disco balls and the changing light patterns of the Institute du Monde Arabe in Paris inspired the focus on changing patterns of light defined by forms.

To explore our ideas, we envisaged an installation featuring an array of tiles that could be moved, or provoked, by the elements. Wind was felt to introduce too much risk to a real-world application, while water did not afford enough variance. With an eye toward the eventual real-world application of our work, we devised an 8 x 8 grid of 64 tiles that would be moved by variances in external temperature. Envisaged as an external screen, the dark coloration was selected to attract more heat into the system, the tiles then moving and responding to external changes in temperature, opening and closing via a series of gas struts. The surface of the individual tiles themselves, designed to catch light combined with the unpredictable response of the system, itself essentially driven by the weather, helps create a dynamic and engaging piece.

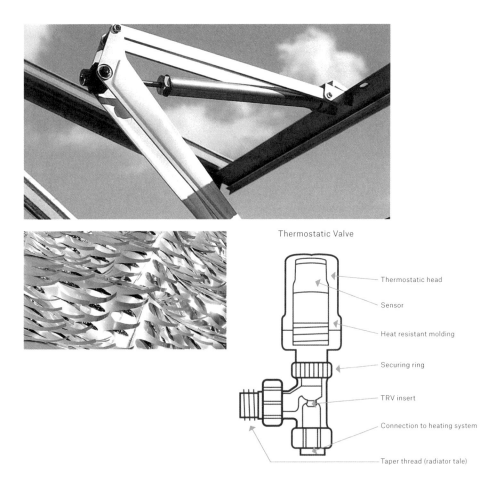

Thermostatic Valve

- Thermostatic head
- Sensor
- Heat resistant molding
- Securing ring
- TRV insert
- Connection to heating system
- Taper thread (radiator tale)

Diagram of a thermostatic valve which is implemented to open the system in response to temperature variations.

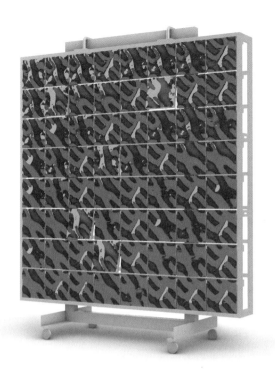

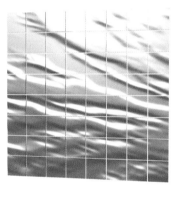

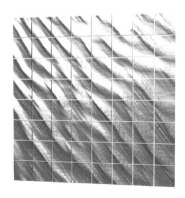

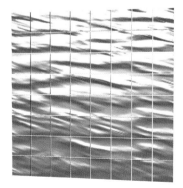

Multiple patterns were designed and deployed across sets of tiles.

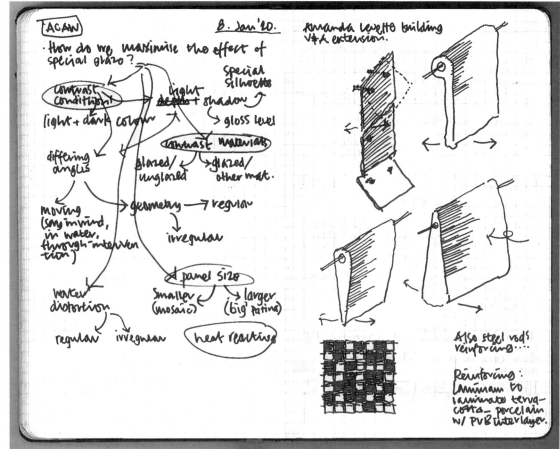

Mock-up of mobile tile assembly.

We studied different ways by which temperature could tilt the assembled tiles and considered methods in which thermo bimetallic strips might move them. To test another option for our design, we built a mock-up that used standard radiator thermostats to prod at the backs of tiles before finally settling on thermo gas struts clamped to the rear of the tiles. The struts would be positioned at varying distances from the back of tiles to allow the advancing strut probes to engage with the tiles (and thus tilt them) at varying spectrums of temperature, adding to the organic impression of the installation. The installation was intended to be produced from commercially available and standardized elements, with tiles pivoting on dowels supported on Unistrut framing.

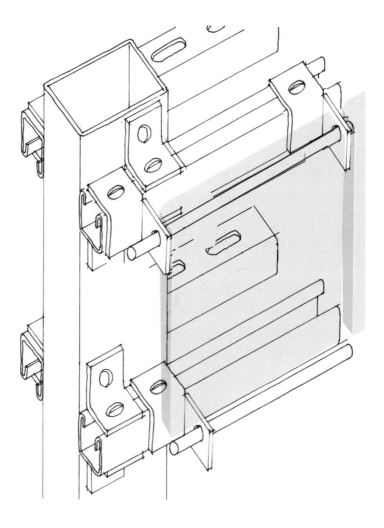

Axonometric drawing of the proposed mechanism.

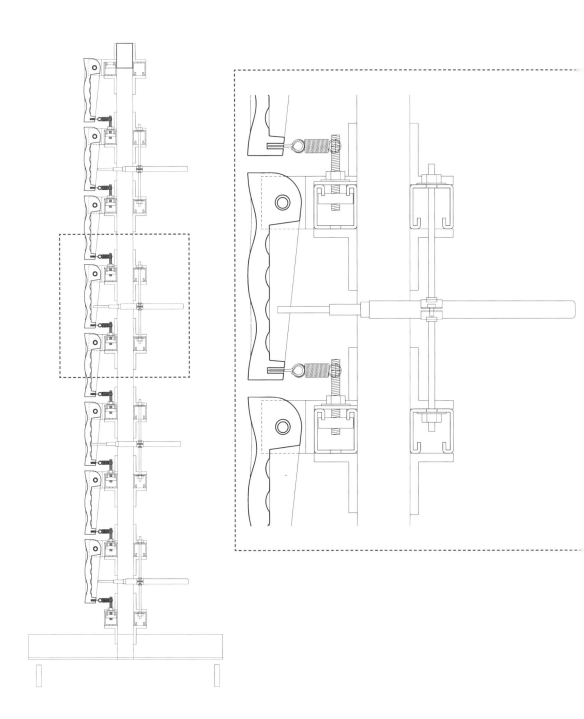

Section of a performative assembly showing tiles and actuators.

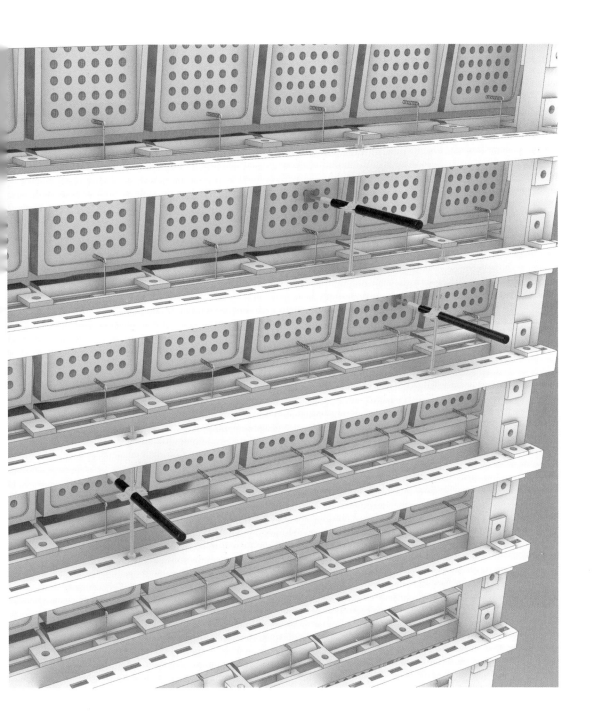

Rendering of the proposed tile assembly.

We then focused our efforts on the composition of the tiles themselves. Rather than including only flat tiles, we hoped the sculpting of the tiles could enhance the effect of movement. We studied patterns drawn from nature, including sand dunes and long marsh grass before settling upon a composition that evoked the rippling of a body of water's surface. Using parametric design we enabled the entire composition to be formed from only 4 tile molds without compromising the visual effect.

Tiles show the light catching on the fluid forms of the surface of the four tile module.

When considering the tile glaze, we focused on glazes that could represent a journey through patina achieved over time or process expressing manufacture, wear, and use. We were interested in precedents such as the cladding on the underside of the Space Shuttle (which achieves a scorched effect when entering the Earth's atmosphere) and the metal on industrial objects which becomes polished or burnished through years of use.

We worked closely with Christine, who tested and sampled many glazes aimed at satisfying our visual aspirations for depth, reflectivity and character from her studio in 's-Hertogenbosch in The Netherlands. The final glaze was a dark blue-black that had a patinated, metallic, almost oily character to it. She devised a glaze recipe that was not only visually effective, but which might also be mass-produced in a cost-effective manner under factory conditions.

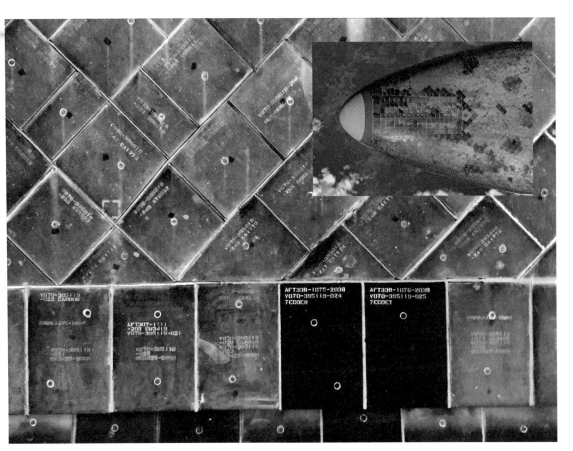

The Space Shuttle is covered by more than 24,000 six- by six-inch blocks resistant up to 2300 degrees Fahrenheit. Image courtesy NASA.

The final step for our process was working with Boston Valley Terra Cotta—together with ceramicist Andy Brayman. We were able to replicate Christine's glaze and then proceeded to full size slip cast tiles with glaze applied to both front and back. The resulting tile had real sculptural character and depth within the glaze since it registers quite differently according to the viewing angle and direction of light.

Full size tile mock up front and inside views.

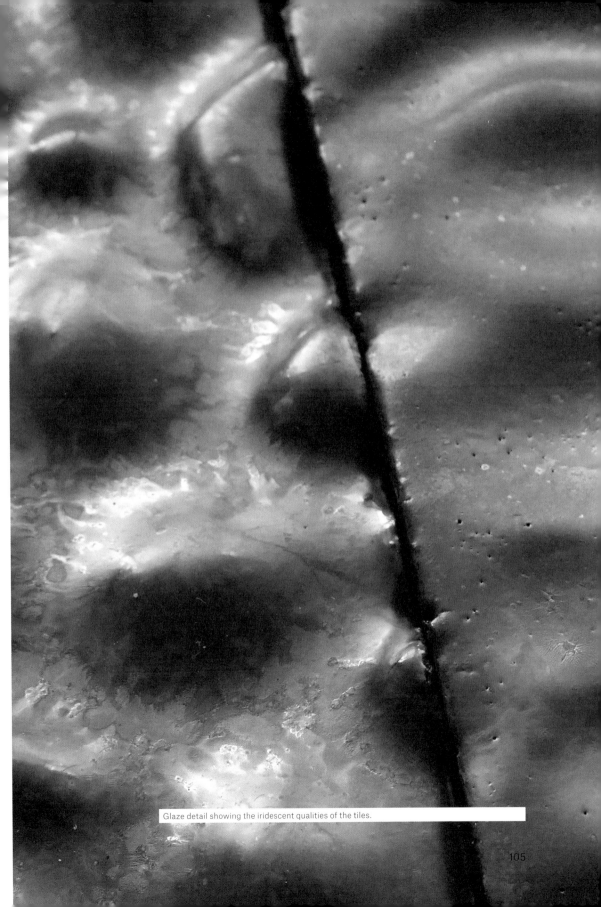

Glaze detail showing the iridescent qualities of the tiles.

Variation in surface and color is produced by orientation of each tile and its relation to the light source and the viewer.

Screen

Volumetric Isohedrals

LMN Architects / Walter P Moore

Project team

LMN Architects	Alex Woodhouse AIA *(Team coordinator)*
	Associate
	Stephen Van Dyck AIA
	Partner
	Scott Crawford
	Principal
	Evgeniya Plotnikova AIA
	Associate
	Hank Butitta
	Designer, Fabrication
Walter P Moore	Soheil Mohommedi SE
	Principle, Structures
	Norman Richardson
	Specialty Structures Engineer
	Laura Karnath
	Enclosure Technical Designer
Architect	Plamena Milusheva
University at Buffalo School of Architecture and Planning	James Renda
	Graduate Student Assistant
	Jacob Barkan
	Graduate Student Assistant
	Brian Nicpon
	Graduate Student Assistant

LMN approached ACAW 2020 as an opportunity to re-interpret traditional methods of craft while leveraging contemporary work-flows. We were interested in how 21st century tools and methods of production embrace the tactile elegance of terracotta while connecting it with environmental and biophilic practices. Ornamental expression was enhanced by introducing a performative aspect to the project: we sought to re-position terracotta from cladding-centric applications to a stand-alone assembly capable of supporting its own bioclimatic-informed programmatic opportunities.

With these objectives in mind, we discovered interrelated families of focused research based on material applications, production techniques and performance limitations. These families—repetitive aggregation, solid/void adjacencies, volumetric modules—were pursued individually for much of the concept phase. Upon concluding this phase, key elements of these tangential studies coalesced, resulting in a hybrid volumetric slip cast module.

When aggregated, the singular module manifests as a self-supporting, thickened wall assembly. This porous assembly is contextually programmable, with disparate, site-specific functions driven by project locale, such as implementation as an evaporative cooling partition in arid climates, a vegetated open-air screen supporting lush growth in urban environments, or an earthen site wall promoting biodiversity in landscape applications. Although the project offers

Front, back, and side elevations of a typical module. Initially using the small openings on front/back surfaces for introduction and removal of liquid slip, dashed linework indicates variable face opening at the discretion of the ceramist, interjecting an artisan aspect to an otherwise heavily manufactured process.

Outward face of ceramic module with prototype crawling glaze. All modules were cast from the same slip cast mold, with variation achieved through hand-trimming of the circular opening.

one solution, variation of ceramic volume, color and texture would all contribute to bespoke installations addressing individual needs.

Due to slip casting's labor-intensive mold-making process, a single mold would be fabricated for the purposes of prototyping. As a result, LMN sought a dynamic, irregular geometry to visually undermine the project's repetitive nature. This visual complexity from a singular element became a focal point of our research as we considered how to aggregate modules into an architectural wall assembly.

Initially referencing 2D tiling of pure-tessellation geometries (equilateral triangles, squares, and equilateral hexagons) resulted in overly predictable, commonplace patterns, and lacked a richness in visual expression. The team adopted the p31m isohedral tiling method (same-shape pattern comprised of 3-fold rotations, reflections, and glide-reflections) as our underlying geometric logic. Unlike pure-tessellation geometries, the irregular baseline geometry

Unfired slip cast before the neck is cut to create a unique opening in each component.

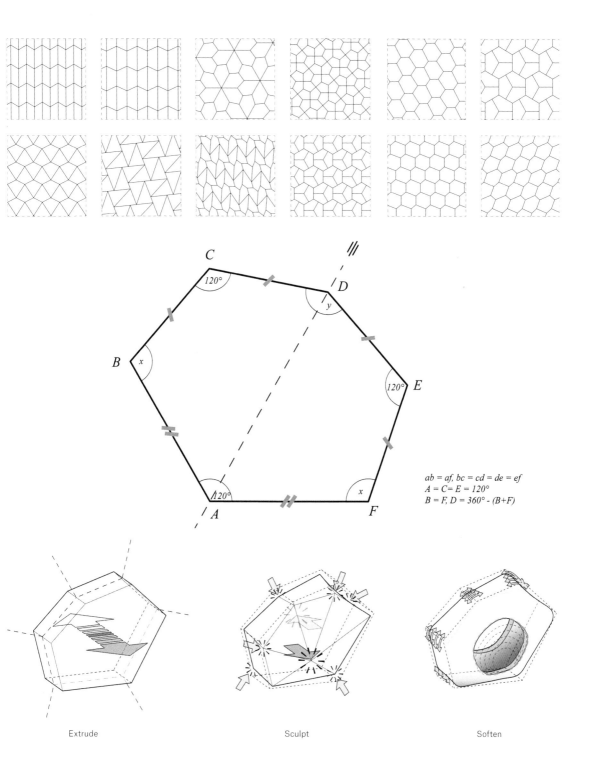

$$ab = af, bc = cd = de = ef$$
$$A = C = E = 120°$$
$$B = F, D = 360° - (B+F)$$

Extrude

Sculpt

Soften

At top, examples of regular and semiregular isohedral tilings of a 2D plane. At middle, the team identified the 109° variant of the p31m geometry as its underlaying mathematical basis, described as shown. At bottom, the p31m geometry was thickened into a volume and sculpted to its completed form.

and related asymmetrical tiling sequence belie the simplicity that a singular profile can attain. The unit was then defined by the resulting 2D tile boundary which was literally thickened and sculpted to provide a volumetric module.

The interstitial void between modules presented another critical design moment. With dry-stack aggregation not permitted due to safety concerns, the team opted to variably increase this perimeter void, introducing a secondary element as spacer within the larger ceramic framework. The fixed dimensions, impermeability and hardness of glazed terracotta suggested that a softer, compressible material would work well in providing adjustability and tolerance, which led to the use of silicone. These spacers are cast from three unique molds to connect the repetitive (but varied) ceramic modules. Each mold is composed of four 3D-printed parts that nest together. After

An initial assembly of three modules allowed the team to test compressible spacers and rigid hardware connections. Lessons learned were applied to the final assembly, including adjustments to the final spacer design and glazing technique.

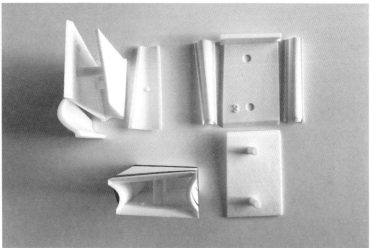

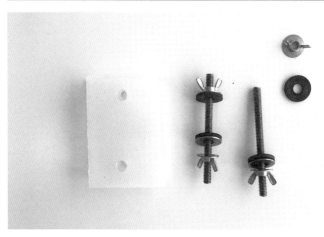

In addition to production of ceramic modules, the team designed and fabricated interstitial compressive spacers made of a mid-hardness silicone. These spacers were inserted between ceramic modules and fastened with a hardware assembly of steel threaded rod, rubber and steel washers, and steel wingnuts.

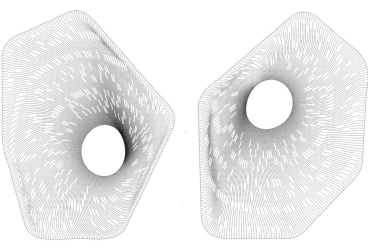

Retaining the mold-positive production process afforded the team another design element in development of the surface texture. This texture, in combination with glazing technique, became the aesthetic identity of the project. At top, linework that generated final CNC finishing operation. At middle and bottom, images of the CNC milling operation, where the ball end mill finishing pass became integral to surface texture of the high-density foam.

experimenting with multiple levels of silicone compressibility, a mid-range hardness was selected for production. The organic nature of silicone paradoxically contrasts with the enduring imagery of terracotta, highlighting a future track for research focused on the connective tissue of these assemblies.

Fabrication being an ongoing research initiative at LMN, participation in the production process was not simply desired, but embedded into the project's DNA. Although unable to assist in the slip casting or glazing processes, LMN sought control of production of the mold-positives, both as means of fully understanding the production sequence as well as identifying additional design opportunities inherent in the process. One such opportunity was the finishing texture. Knowing LMN would be CNC milling high-density foam for the mold-positive, we iterated 3D linework topologies, celebrating the finish milling operation as an extra layer of filigree on the module surface. In the end, a contoured dashing pattern was selected, for both its independent appearance, as well as how it manifested after glazing. Working with a 3-axis machine complicated this process (specifically at edge conditions between horizontal/vertical faces), but ultimately resulted in a more intriguing digital texture that only the most ardent digital technicians would recognize.

Up until this point, much of the project was computationally derived, from initial geometry to surface texturing, mold-making, and spacer development. The team was interested in uniting past and present in the final object while interjecting playfulness into an otherwise heavily manufactured process. We desired an analog expression, something that would lend an element of handcrafted finesse while contributing to the unique representation of each individual unit. Prior to glazing the wet-state ceramic, the two outward faces of each terracotta module were carved by hand, resulting in variable-sized openings. In doing so, every module adopted a distinct identity within the overall composition.

With assistance from Walter P. Moore's Specialty Structures team, LMN's design was investigated from two interconnected vantage points: how an individual module would translate compressive loads within its geometry, and how interconnected modules would distribute compressive forces throughout a wall assembly. Due to the variable nature of hand-carved outward faces on individual modules,

finite element analysis was performed for a worst-case scenario of only the "waist geometry" (derived from the 2D tile boundary). This analysis was informative, prompting us to relocate hardware connections from waist edges, where stresses are highest, to mid-waist faces, which not only reduced stress on the ceramic but also created more expressive and dynamic interstitial spaces between modules.

Referencing the assembly, the engineers simulated how compression would translate through an aggregation of units, and where gravity loads would be most severe. These simulations informed ceramic thickness (¾" target), hardware capacity, and structural capacity of a full aggregation (723 psi bearing capacity with 6x Factor of Safety would yield a continuous wall 12 units tall) which in turn dictated the unit topology.

As a fundamental aesthetic quality of architectural terracotta, the LMN team took considerable interest in the development of glaze expression and color. Glazes were studied in tandem with surface texture, with the intent that these two variables express a "digital/ organic" language. Color was explored as an accent that would complement design features while being passive on waist surfaces. In the

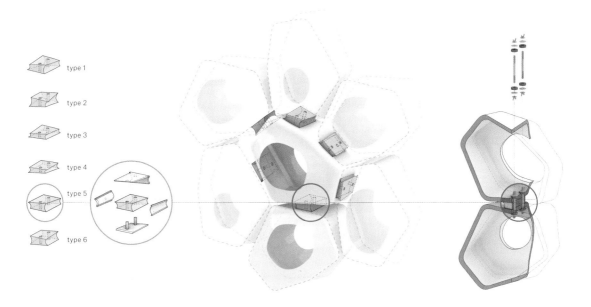

type 1
type 2
type 3
type 4
type 5
type 6

Observing a typical module, six spacers and accompanying hardware are required to situate this unit within the overall assembly. At left, the three spacer types (front and back views) and exploded view of one spacer and its mold. At right, module section showing installation of hardware through modules and spacer.

end, the team selected a gradient crawling glaze that was responsive to the underlying toolpath while exhibiting a distinct effect all its own.

The LMN project was assembled on-site at Boston Valley in early November 2020. Although a 3-module test assembly was performed in LMN's shop, the full installation highlighted lessons revealed by the project that can drive further development. Building upon ACAW 2020 investigations, future development of this project would prioritize three fundamental aspects of architectural

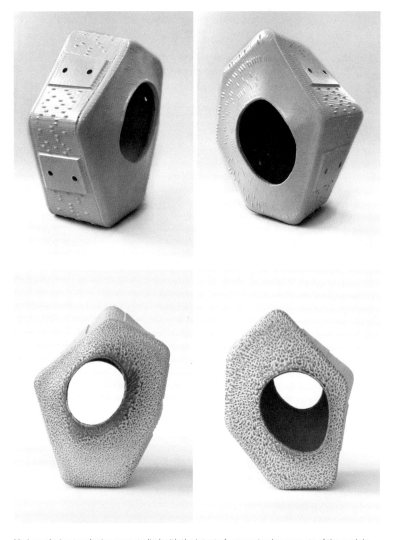

Various glazing typologies were studied with the intent of expressing key aspects of the module design. At top, a gradient glaze highlighted surface inflection and the hand-carved detailing. At bottom, a crawling glaze complimented the milled surface texture of the module. The final glaze embraced both ideas, resulting in a gradient crawling glaze responsive yet independent of the surface texture below.

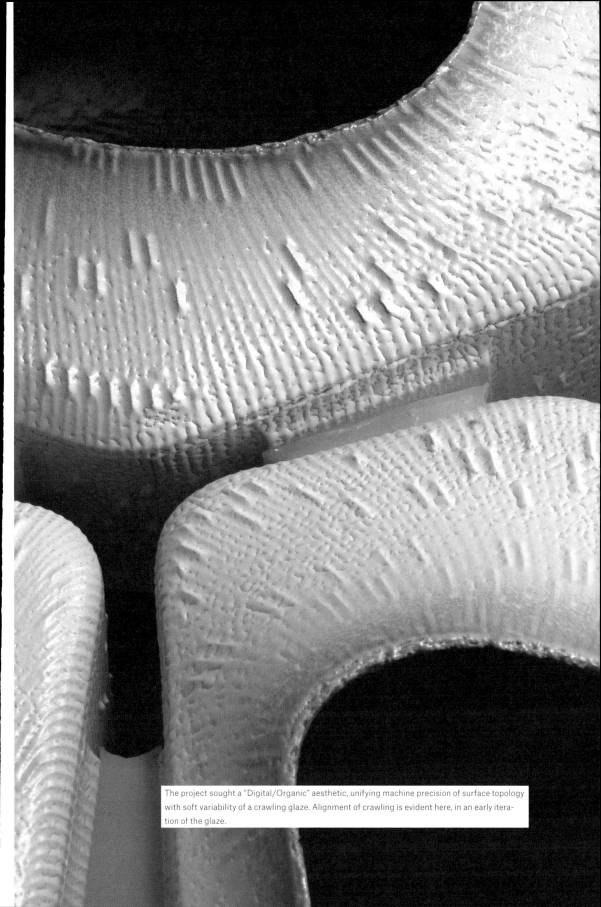

The project sought a "Digital/Organic" aesthetic, unifying machine precision of surface topology with soft variability of a crawling glaze. Alignment of crawling is evident here, in an early iteration of the glaze.

terracotta that embrace the modularity and craft of production: streamlined fabrication, texture/glaze synergies, and compatibility of ancillary components.

The project's singular module taught us the limitations and affordances of the slip casting process. Principally, mass production with a slip cast mold is prohibitive due to the labor involved. This leads us to consider alternative production techniques such as ram pressing, which would in turn offer different (i.e., non-undercut) geometries to our volumetric module. The project also offered many lessons in the duality of texture and glaze, but left much additional investigation on the table. With the final surface treatment as a starting point, continued investigation of texture, glaze, and casting orientation would likely offer results that respond to or augment the qualities of the bioclimatic context as well.

Material longevity of the ceramic modules and related componentry present another interesting exploration, particularly as we seek to build with more sustainable practices. On the one hand, the project could simply identify spacer materials compatible with the lifespan of terracotta. Perhaps more interestingly, the assembly could be engineered such that, across decades, a combined settling of modules and natural deposition of organic matter could relieve the silicone spacers of their structural duties, further connecting the assembly to its context.

The completed assembly showcases eleven modules within a plywood and steel framework. Plywood nuggets replicate ceramic modules while providing adjustable attachment to underlaying structural support.

At scale, the project proposes a porous wall of indeterminate length, contextually located and programmed to accommodate a variety of uses—evaporative cooling partition in arid climates, vegetated open-air screen supporting lush growth, or earthen site wall promoting biodiversity.

Surface texture is defined by a combination of glaze and detailing of the form.

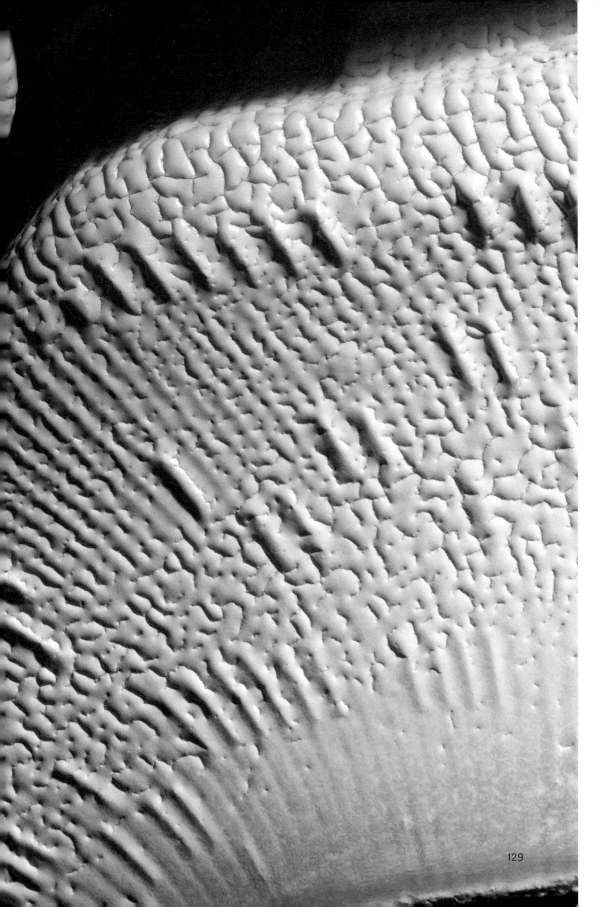

129

Polyvalent Pixel: an Aggregate of Form

Adrian Smith + Gordon Gill Architecture

Project team

Adrian Smith + Gordon Gill Architecture	Anthony Viola AIA *(Team coordinator)* *Architect* Hiram Rodriguez *Design Technologist* Nicholas Berchtold *Fabrication Lead*
Thornton Tomasetti	Charles Portelli AIA *Senior Associate—Computational Designer* Silverio Patrizi *Senior Associate—Façade Engineering* Amandine Cersosimo *Senior Façade Engineer*
University at Buffalo School of Architecture and Planning	Carlos Cuadrado *Student Assistant* Jonathan Harris *Student Assistant*

Our investigation for ACAW 2020 focused on augmenting architectural terra cotta for enhanced performance. The intended augmentations targeted:

1. reducing embodied carbon in manufacturing and deployment

2. increasing component performance through material logic and parametric modeling in terms of VOC/carbon sequestration, thermal performance, daylight harvesting, improved structural performance and reduced energy consumption, and

3. embedding technology into the terra cotta assemblies to increase occupant comfort and monitor and modulate whole building performance to adapt to dynamic environmental conditions, such as changes in air quality, shifts in occupancy, ambient lighting conditions, and temperature.

To arrive at our prototype, we simultaneously developed a local component or "pixel" as well as the global aggregate assembly system, which was tuned for specific environmental conditions.

The team found inspiration in two historical systems, Guastavino-style tile domes and early-20th century structural terra cotta blocks, which Boston Valley Terra Cotta brought to our attention. Both systems are highly performative due to a combination of their manufacturing process and unit design, as well as their aggregation technique. Developed in the early 1900s, the structural terra cotta blocks used in fireproofing systems in early steel framed high rises were lighter than traditional masonry and could be configured into different geometries and integrated into different building systems. The specific shape, surface treatment or keys, and voids allowed the units to be used in vertical or horizontal applications to be load bearing or cladding. The Guastavino tiles and the vaulted forms that they create were another important reference where a simple repeatable cell or "pixel" is configured into an efficient aggregate system, a thin vault with minimal material usage. This was particularly inspiring to the team.

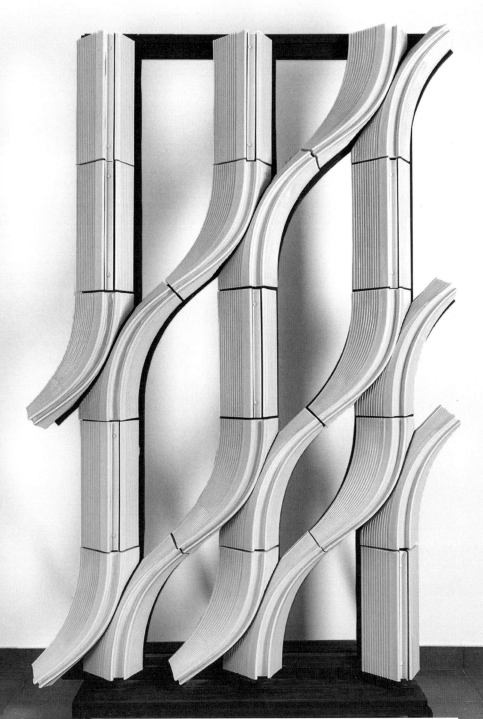

Unit assembly at 35 percent of scale shows the modular pattern and form expression.

At one of the smallest scales investigated, early design studies analyzed the functionality of a titanium dioxide (TiO_2) coating material for its photocatalytic VOC/smog eating function. As the intense heat of firing the ceramic mutes the photocatalytic properties of the TiO_2 materials, the team explored application of cold and warm TiO_2 coatings to glazed and un-glazed fired architectural terra cotta panels. The material application was coupled with an investigation of various surface textures that increase the surface area exposed to the air and sun, and thereby increase the VOC/smog-eating potential of the building elements. The final prototype's texture configuration balanced the size and shape of textural intervention with the limits / constraints of the terra cotta manufacturing technique, which in this case was extrusion. The final texture in the mockup increased the surface area of the individual component by approximately 40 percent which, when coated with a cold applied TiO_2 solution, would increase it's NO_2 "smog eating" potential by that same amount.

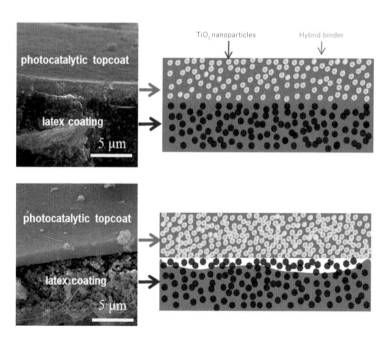

Photo-catalytic TiO_2-based self-cleaning coatings TiO_2 solution,"eats smog" by binding it to the surface it is applied to. © 2017 Elsevier B.V. All rights reserved.

Various surface textures were evaluated to increase the exposed surface area, increasing the photocatalytic efficacy.

As we started to look at the next scale up, the team investigated how the "fluidity" of the raw material during the manufacturing process permits surfaces that can be designed to continuously align their shape for different structural conditions. Several early design studies explored how changing the bending axis of the terra cotta component increases the system rigidity and ultimately reduces the amount of required structural material. As expressed in the asymmetrical rake of our prototype wall, the unique manufacturing process also means that components could be customized to transition a vertical shade to horizontal shade for better solar performance or potential energy harvesting. As the individual components aggregate, their rhythm and configuration or twisting can be optimized to site and environmentally specific conditions. The manufacturing process and material allows for modulation of the wall opacity, which can affect window-to-wall ratio, spatial daylight autonomy, and the management of views.

The team explored these permutations by using a visual scripting platform (Rhino/Grasshopper) to develop an integrated parametric model, the tools allow us to build a multilayered script which tracks various inputs and parameters that are key for overall design performance. Our main focus was to achieve low embodied carbon, so the parametric model needed to include typical façade system components as well as the terra cotta components. As this was envisioned to improve wall performance, we integrated thermal properties as well as operational energy inputs such as grid energy and typical energy loads for each scenario. Using Wallace, an evolutionary solver for Grasshopper, we were able to run about 1000 variations which helped inform our design process.

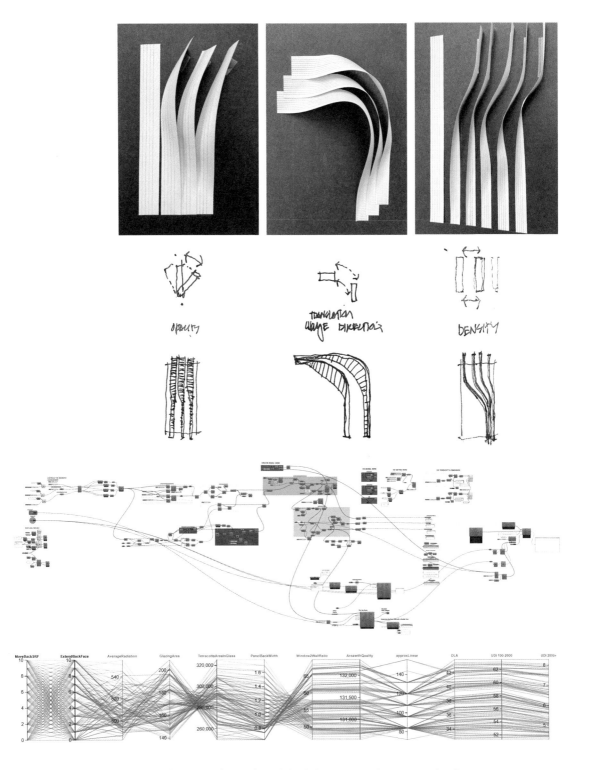

Early paper strip form studies and sketch showing various density twist and configuration parameters (above) were followed by smart form design script defining generation and embodied carbon analysis (below).

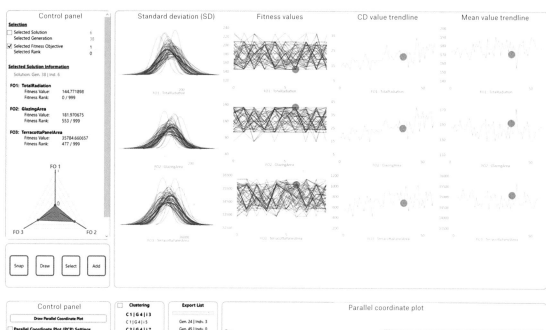

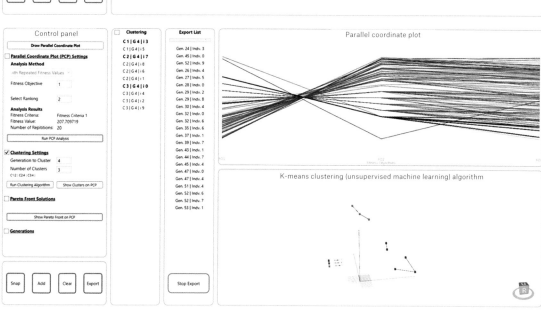

Wallace fitness UI shows various result from our design script. The tool allows for clustering using K-Means (Unsupervised Machine Learning) which help select our form based on perfomance.

TERRACOTTA X PROFILES
Deflections

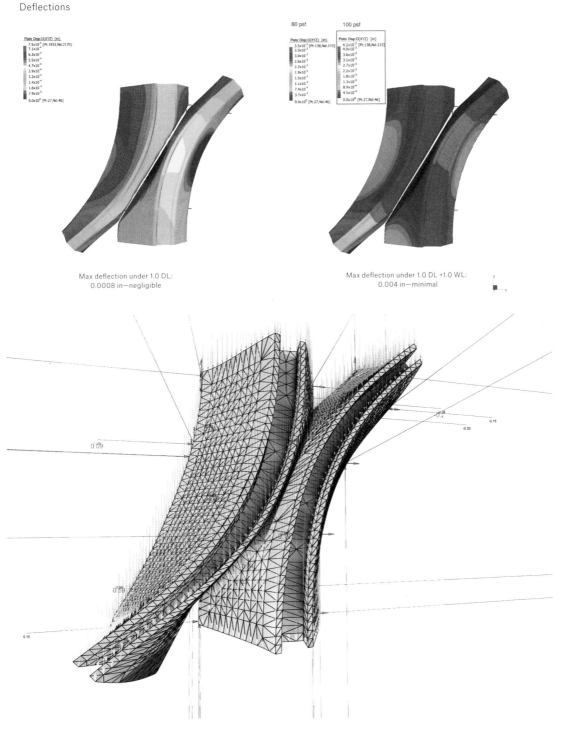

Max deflection under 1.0 DL:
0.0008 in—negligible

Max deflection under 1.0 DL +1.0 WL:
0.004 in—minimal

The analysis of the X Profile conducted by Thornton Tomasetti, FEA, shows negligible to minimal deflection under normal to high stress conditions.

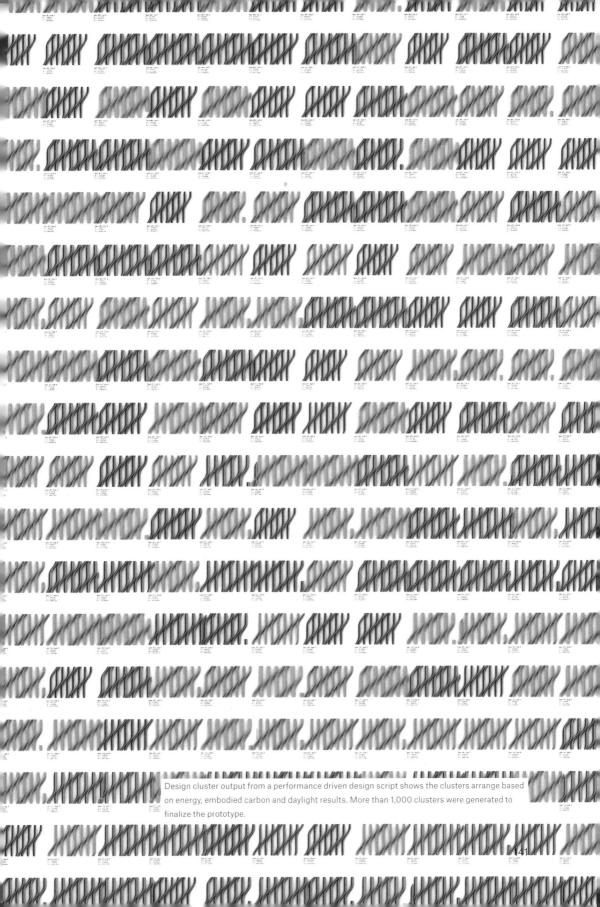

Design cluster output from a performance driven design script shows the clusters arrange based on energy, embodied carbon and daylight results. More than 1,000 clusters were generated to finalize the prototype.

The results provided a large data set which we could benchmark and classify for various building profiles and orientations. For example, the shape configuration of our façade prototype could transform in the X, Y, Z direction to allow for maximum daylight while producing the lowest overall lifecycle carbon. Finally, when we integrated manufacturing logic the team found that having a higher variation of extruded forms (changing lengths) and lower variation of molded or cast pieces (which require unique molds) would perform best from a system cost standpoint. The prototype assembly represents a single condition optimized for a typical wall on the eastern facade of a theoretical building located in Chicago.

Close up view of the X Profile prototype assembly.

BASE LINE DESIGN

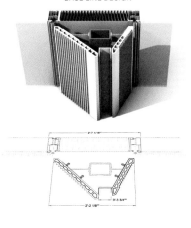

OPTION 1

OPTION 2

OPTION 3

OPTION 4

Rhino3d mock-ups of various connection details were use to inform early feasibility studies.

The team has determined several avenues for further research related to the augmentation and integration of the smart façade to internal building performance. The current design integrates IOT sensors to track environmental factors such as indoor and outdoor temperature and humidity, as well as building occupancy and indoor air quality. This distributed sensor array is at a much finer grain and, when integrated into a Smart Building Management System, can more accurately react to live sensor data and reduce the overall building operational carbon. The "responsiveness" of the architectural elements could also be digital, and early AR/XR tools used during the workshop could be developed into deeper integrations where building occupants can visualize these data points on a dashboard or through their smartphone utilizing a QR code embedded into the façade. Future "smart" façades can have more intelligent sensors which communicate with the digital devices of building occupants and inform them of unseen environmental conditions – something at the forefront of current discussions in the design of post-pandemic buildings and cities. Additionally, we recognized that the embedded carbon footprint and energy use of the electronics vs the potential energy savings is something that would have to be investigated, but was out of the scope of this study.

Finally, further refinement and investigation is intended to compare the total lifecycle carbon of this type of composite system to other façade systems, such as wood, concrete, etc., of similar configurations. The design as presented is a single condition and is optimized for that condition, but the framework/process is agnostic and has the flexibility to adapt and adjust to any environment and location to which we apply it. Such adaptability allows the design to do more with less lifecycle carbon, both embedded and operational, and will make future designs smarter and more globally environmentally responsible.

Continuous light ribbon
rgb led strip
individually addressable led
exterior neopixel variant

Sensor
exterior environmental sensor array
bosch bme680 mox type sensor
senses level of voc in surrounding air
breakout temp, humidity, voc levels
fusioned aqi

Controller
arduino uno/mega 5v
cycles the indivisually addressed leds
with chosen reporting visualization

Sensor
exterior environmental sensor array
bosch bme680 mox type sensor
senses level of voc in surrounding air
breakout temp, humidity, voc levels
fusioned aqi

Controller
arduino uno/mega 5v
cycles the indivisually addressed leds
with chosen reporting visualization

Continuous light ribbon
rgbw led strip
individually addressable led
exterior neopixel variant

Sensor
exterior environmental sensor array
bosch bme680 mox type sensor
senses level of voc in surrounding air
breakout temp, humidity, voc levels
fusioned aqi

Controller
arduino uno/mega 5v
cycles the indivisually addressed leds
with chosen reporting visualization

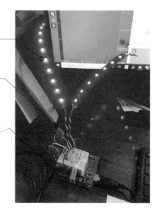

Embedded sensor array systems augment the design with environmental inputs.

Deep section of the X Profile assembly.

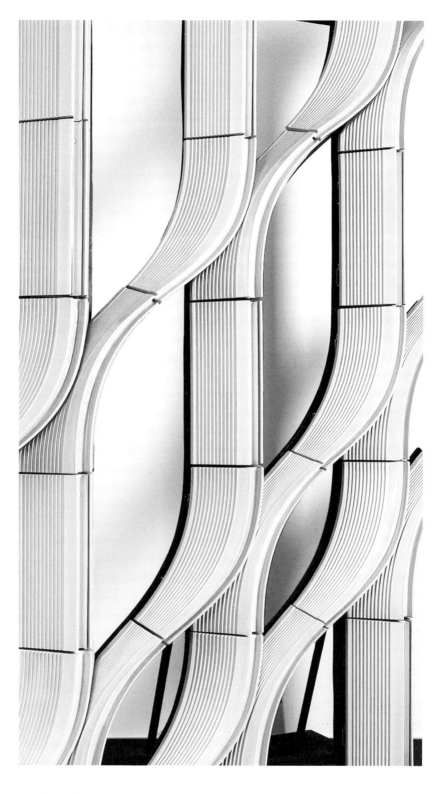

X Profile assembly.

Fish Scale Screen

Handel Architects

Project team

Handel Architects	Gary Handel *Managing Partner* Paul Lenke *Associate* Jonathan Morefield *Associate* Stefan Di Leo *Associate Architect* Noah Rosenberg *Architectural Designer*
DeSimone Consulting Engineers	Alex Barmas *Senior Associate* Whitney Boykin *Associate* Rok Lee *Principal*

The Handel team merged two distinct lines of inquiry in their investigations into architectural terra cotta assemblies. The first was driven by an interest in innovating the assembly system, and related to the means for developing a flexible exterior building cladding system with terra cotta. The second was driven by our focus on sustainable building futures, and addressed whether one of the world's oldest building materials could be rethought for exterior cladding in a way that would support the industry's efforts to combat climate change. These two tracks coalesced in the development of a support system for the assembly, with the exploration of the terra cotta unit itself being driven by the optical effects inspired by the fluidity and iridescence of biological models.

The team explored a number of ways to organize and support the facade system such that it maintained the functional and aesthetic fluidity, while reducing material and energy intensive aluminum components to a minimum. Ultimately, we settled on a cable net that uses tension to capture the terra cotta units within it. This provides the flexibility that the team desired, with the rigid terra cotta units functioning as nodes in the wire net, which can be deployed within different configurations due to the inherent flexure of a net structure.

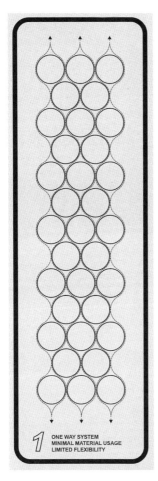

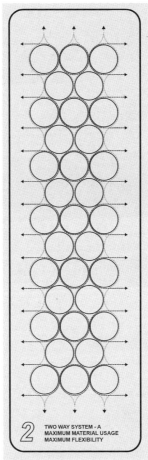

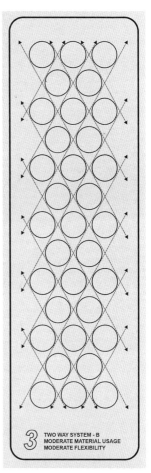

1 ONE WAY SYSTEM
MINIMAL MATERIAL USAGE
LIMITED FLEXIBILITY

2 TWO WAY SYSTEM - A
MAXIMUM MATERIAL USAGE
MAXIMUM FLEXIBILITY

3 TWO WAY SYSTEM - B
MODERATE MATERIAL USAGE
MODERATE FLEXIBILITY

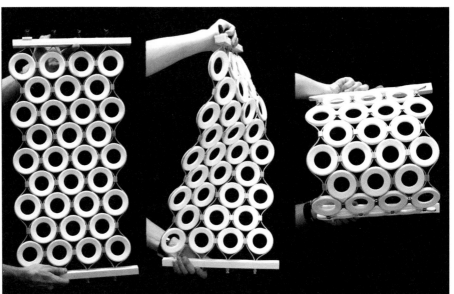

Diagrams and study models of the tensile net concept.

The front of the prototype assembly with the glazed terracotta units (top). The backside of the prototype assembly with the tensile cable system (bottom).

In developing this solution, we explored systems that held the units between wires and ones that threaded the wires through the units, before settling on the latter. Working in collaboration with DeSimone Consulting Engineers, we evaluated two main tensile net structures: a 1-way gravity loaded tensile system, and a 2-way pre-tensioned tensile system. After investigation and development of both systems, we found that the 2-way system was a much better fit for exterior applications. The 2-way system allowed us to drastically reduce the amount of aluminum and the number of contact points through the thermal/moisture barrier of the building exterior. Limiting the metal components was a priority, since the high embodied energy of aluminum augments the sustainability possibilities of terra cotta's comparatively low embodied energy. This strategy also simplifies the assembly process reducing cost associated with labor.

For the ACAWorkshop prototype assembly, we developed a solution that used off-the-shelf hardware. The mechanism uses a 2-way cable clamp to which the terra cotta units are attached at varying angles using preset eye-end bolts. Further engineering of the cable system would move towards a customized solution that requires less components and materials, since reduction of metal components is critical to the team's sustainability goals.

Perhaps the most exciting discovery was the system's ability to be manipulated into more complex ruled surfaces. The ruled surfaces created an ordering system for the cablenet. This encouraged the team to explore how we can use the system geometry and the shape of the terra cotta component to further enhance its sustainable characteristics. The shaping of the surface could provide varying degrees of thermal absorption as demonstrated by our simulations.

Biomimicry also inspired two aspects of the project: the form of the terra cotta units and the glazing strategy. In the development of the final geometry, we were inspired by the skin of reptiles. We were interested not only in the texture, but in the potential of replicating the protective and performative functions of the reptiles' scaled skin. The biomimetic model drove us to pursue a shingled/scaled shape for the terra cotta units that allowed the design to shed wind and water like a traditional rain screen cladding system.

The light-scattering effects in the wings of butterflies and the exoskeletons of beetles inspired the glazing design. We worked closely with Andy Brayman of The Matter Factory to deconstruct the color-shifting phenomenon that initially captivated us. After weeks of experimentation we honed-in on two distinct iridescent glazes. The primary glaze is a dark green color at its base and color-shifts with view-angle to a metallic bronze when viewed in the oblique. The secondary glaze is more opalescent and subtle, preserving the visibility of the clay body underneath. As the light source moves, the thin iridescent coating obscures the base tones to create a rich otherworldly landscape on the vertical building surface.

The organization and form of fish scales was of particular interest.

Modules with the iridescent glazing developed with The Matter Factory.

Once the unit and cable net design were set, the development of the assembly focused on interaction with daylight. This was accomplished through the rotation of the terra cotta scales in the tensile cable system. One of the major breakthroughs in the design development process was the realization that by pivoting or rotating the terra cotta "scale," we could dilate the system to create transparency in the façade; bringing light into the interior spaces where glazing is provided. Not only could this be achieved within the cable net system, but with a single scale through rotation. This allowed the assembly to be visually dynamic, since each ram-pressed scale's distinct orientation will make it appear to have a different form than those adjacent to it. Due to this rotational possibility, the same unit could make an assembly that functions as closed rain screen cladding or an open brise soleil screen.

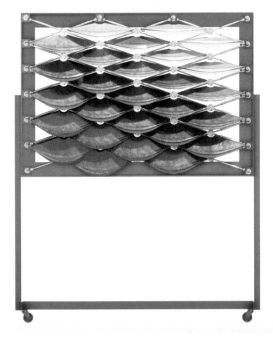

Rendered representation of the final prototype assembly.

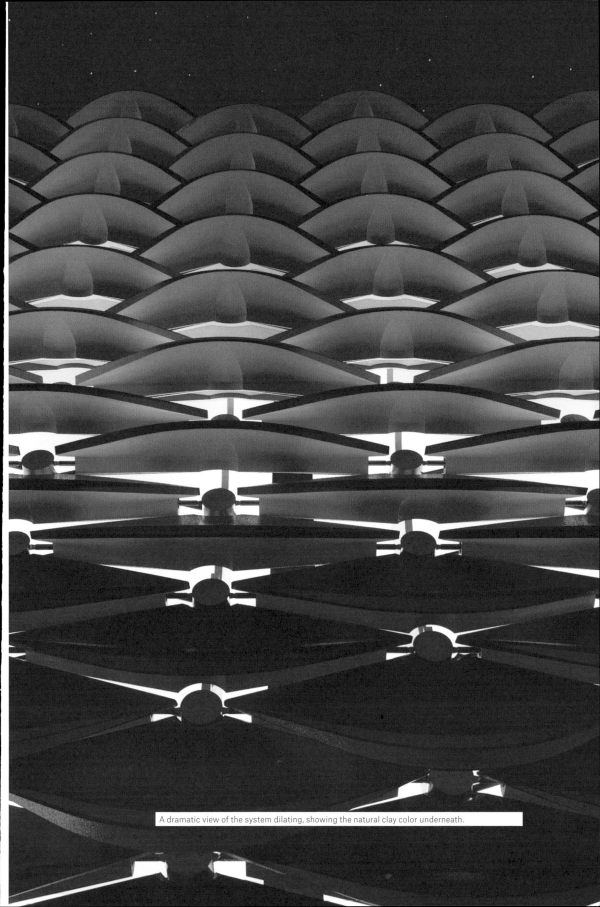

A dramatic view of the system dilating, showing the natural clay color underneath.

Initially, we proposed fabricating the pieces using the slip cast method, which involves pouring liquid clay into a plaster mold. This is commonly used to produce bespoke or one of a kind units especially those that are to be seen in the round. But since our intention is that this component could be produced for large facade applications, the final terra cotta "scale" module was designed to be ram-pressed, which facilitates production at an industrial scale. When ram-pressing, the clay body is placed in-between two sculpted molds. As the press activates, the top mold presses downward into the bottom mold compacting the clay into the desired shape. Minor post-processing is then done to hollow out the pieces to accommodate the attachment hardware. The double sided nature of the ram-press altered the design of the unit to accommodate specific draft angles and the possible duality of the two faces of each component, giving a distinct inside and outside face to the design.

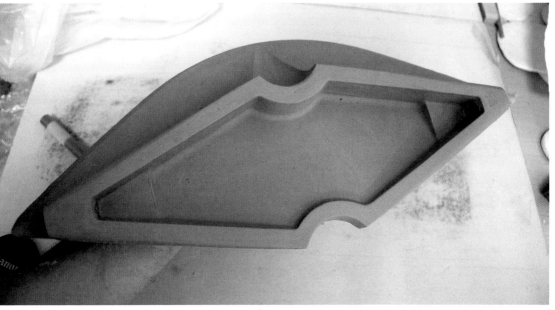

Back (top) and front (bottom) of the ram-pressed terracotta module.

Through the process we studied the geometry through multiple itera-
tions and consulted scientists, engineers, and ceramicists on possible
solutions. Approaches we studied included photocatalytic air filtration,
organic solar PV glazing, green walls and rainwater collection, as well
as exterior wall cavity ventilation. The ACAW prototype focused on
the potential for ventilation and daylight access through the rotation
system and reflective quality of the glaze. The other possibilities were
not developed in this iteration, but have inspired further research and
development of components based on the established unit geometry.
These aspirational technologies can be applied to the system in order
to expand the sustainable capabilities of this ancient material. Our
team is interested in pursuing these avenues of exploration, particularly those centered on the potential of the surface and its glaze to
provide ecosystem services, such as air filtration and energy capture,
without compromising one of the more sustainable aspects of terracotta, its sustainability.

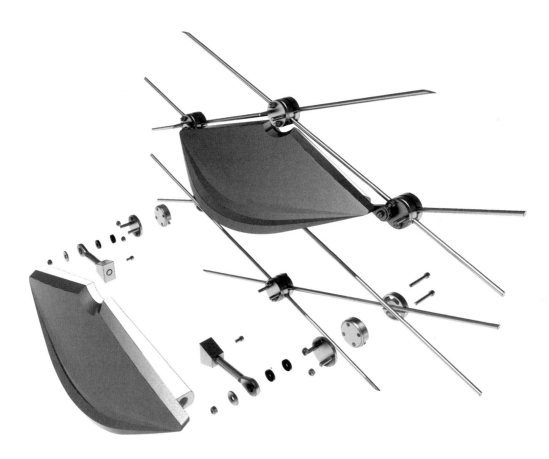

Exploded axonometric of the terracotta module and tensile cable system.

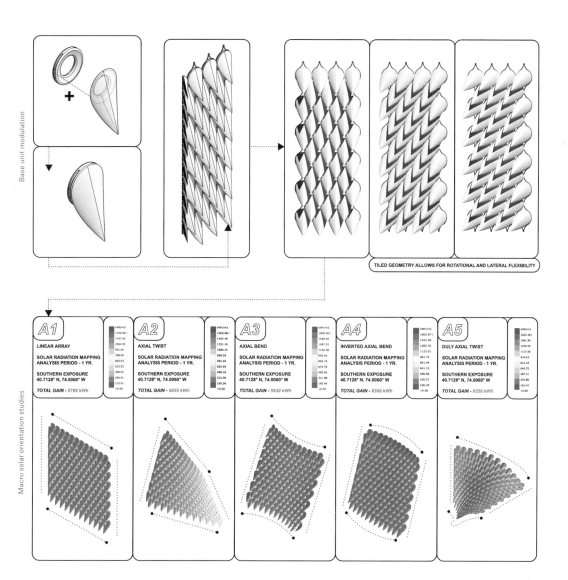

Base unit modulation

Macro solar orientation studies

TILED GEOMETRY ALLOWS FOR ROTATIONAL AND LATERAL FLEXIBILITY

A1

LINEAR ARRAY

SOLAR RADIATION MAPPING
ANALYSIS PERIOD - 1 YR.

SOUTHERN EXPOSURE
40.7128° N, 74.0060° W

TOTAL GAIN - 5789 kWh

kWh/m2
1130.06+
1197.05
2064.95
931.04
798.04
665.03
532.02
398.02
266.01
133.01
<0.00

A2

AXIAL TWIST

SOLAR RADIATION MAPPING
ANALYSIS PERIOD - 1 YR.

SOUTHERN EXPOSURE
40.7128° N, 74.0060° W

TOTAL GAIN - 5655 kWh

kWh/m2
1503.88+
1407.49
1251.10
1094.71
938.33
781.94
625.55
469.16
312.78
156.39
<0.00

A3

AXIAL BEND

SOLAR RADIATION MAPPING
ANALYSIS PERIOD - 1 YR.

SOUTHERN EXPOSURE
40.7128° N, 74.0060° W

TOTAL GAIN - 5830 kWh

kWh/m2
1809.40+
1448.46
1287.52
1126.58
965.64
804.70
643.76
482.82
321.88
160.94
<0.00

A4

INVERTED AXIAL BEND

SOLAR RADIATION MAPPING
ANALYSIS PERIOD - 1 YR.

SOUTHERN EXPOSURE
40.7128° N, 74.0060° W

TOTAL GAIN - 6300 kWh

kWh/m2
1602.87+
1442.58
1282.30
1122.01
961.72
801.44
641.15
480.86
320.57
160.29
<0.00

A5

DULY AXIAL TWIST

SOLAR RADIATION MAPPING
ANALYSIS PERIOD - 1 YR.

SOUTHERN EXPOSURE
40.7128° N, 74.0060° W

TOTAL GAIN - 6250 kWh

kWh/m2
1624.38+
1461.94
1299.50
1137.06
974.63
812.19
649.75
487.31
324.88
162.44
<0.00

Diagrams of the system performance of the tensile net concept.

161

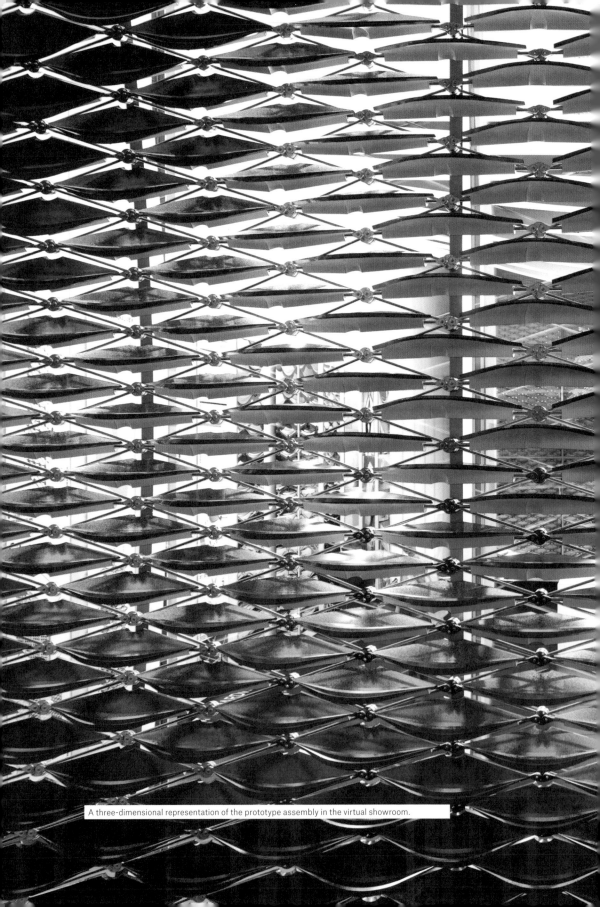

A three-dimensional representation of the prototype assembly in the virtual showroom.

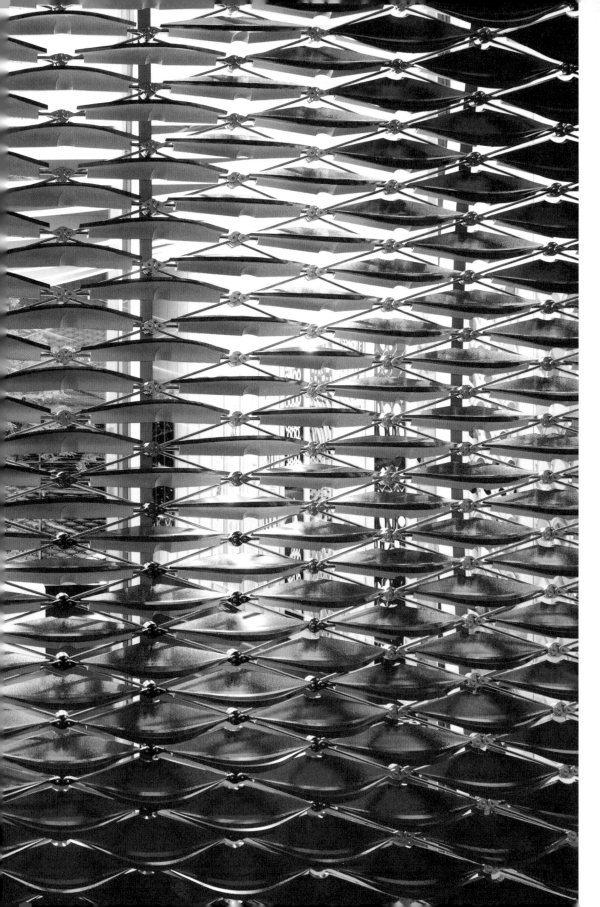

Recasting the Mold

Alfred University/University at Buffalo

Project team

Carnegie Mellon

Laura Garofalo *(Team coordinator)*
Associate Professor

New York State College of
Ceramics at Alfred University,
Division of Ceramic Art

Johnathan Hopp
Assistant Professor
Esme Saccuccimorano, BFA
Nathaniel Hill, BFA

University at Buffalo
School of Architecture
and Planning

Tim Noble
MArch Student

Architectural terra cotta manufacturers have found ways of delivering dynamic compositions of aggregated repetitive units generated from dies and molds. However, these assemblies lack the incremental variability intrinsic to digital morphologies coveted by some contemporary designers. Such assemblies require sets of unique components. A sustainable, digitally driven, cost effective means for producing non-repetitive terra cotta components has proven an elusive goal for manufacturers. Our team's hypothesis is that a system of slip cast molds that adopted cradle to cradle manufacturing practices through efficient instrumentation and material choice, and time saving digital workflow can deliver the coveted assembly of unique units. For ACAW 2020 we developed the Waffle Cast system and produced a prototype of the XBlock screen as proof of concept. The new system not only rethinks the mold by eliminating its waste stream, but allows for morphological variation in the units' production.

Building multiple molds to produce morphological variation is problematic, and even cost prohibitive. Digital manufacturing's promise of mass customization has heretofore been limited by instrumentation and material constraints. In the case of architectural terra cotta, these constraints are not because of the material, but the mold. For centuries, gypsum plaster, as well as bisque fired ceramics, and more recently porous resin, have been used to make these molds. All of these have an ability to absorb moisture from the ceramic slip, thus solidifying it to create a cast shell. Slip casting itself, which is efficient and quick in comparison to other methods, has become increasingly viable due to CNC milling of digital models. However, between the slip cast and the digital drawing there are several labor-intensive and materially wasteful steps—principally the production of single use foam positives. These are not only wasteful, but ecologically degenerative adding to plastic pollution. Digitally milling a plaster mold is possible, but more energy and economically intensive, and the plaster is not recyclable. Consequently, assemblies of completely unique components remain uncommon in the architectural terra cotta industry despite the potential of digital milling.

CBlock units were assembled by team members following the numbering etched on each mold by the laser cutter.

Knowing slip casting can facilitate such assemblies, our team's goal was to eliminate the drawbacks of the mold. Team member Johnathan Hopp had pioneered a process to produce digitally designed sculptural ceramic vessels that swaps the caustic mold materials for absorptive paper, and the CNC mill for a laser cutter. Using chipboard, a material that is not only recyclable, but made of 100 percent recycled fibers, our task was to transform the means of production of a sculptural vessel to that for manufacturing an architectural component.

To achieve this, we needed to create a system that:

— matched the consistent absorptive capabilities of the traditional molds

— scaled the components to industry standards for strength and stability

— provided precision and stability of form necessary for aggregated assemblies

— created a digital workflow that translates the geometry (or positive) into formwork.

Our team developed the Waffle Cast System by working on two fronts: physical testing and scripting a translation from a bespoke geometry to a laser cut mold.

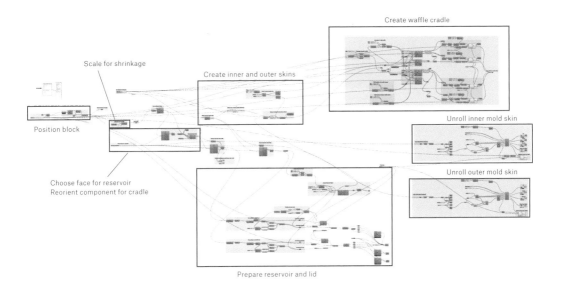

Scale for shrinkage

Create inner and outer skins

Create waffle cradle

Position block

Unroll inner mold skin

Choose face for reservoir
Reorient component for cradle

Unroll outer mold skin

Prepare reservoir and lid

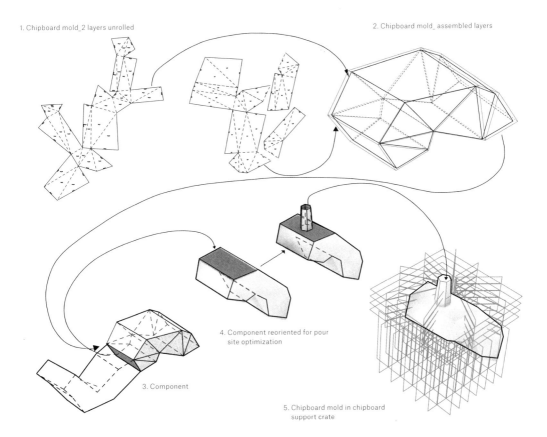

1. Chipboard mold_2 layers unrolled

2. Chipboard mold_ assembled layers

4. Component reoriented for pour
site optimization

3. Component

5. Chipboard mold in chipboard
support crate

The workflow was defined by a set of Grasshopper algorithms which produced the mold and its
structural waffle crate.

Physical tests aimed to increase the scale and precision of casting in chipboard and form the requisite homogeneous ¼ inch thick shell. Initially we cast in 3 inch cubes, which were cut open to expose the shell's makeup and determine the duration of the cast phase. Once this was deemed satisfactory, deformation of the shell and the chipboard were assessed by testing larger cubes to failure. This developed formwork resistant to the weight of liquid clay.

The tests defined:

— the organization and density of the chipboard scaffold,

— the addition of a second layer of chipboard for rigidity, and

— the alignment of folded and open seams between the chipboard layers to prevent leakage and deformation.

The physical tests informed the automation of flat-cut chipboard formwork patterns configurable to multiple geometries. A form can easily be unrolled in a rhino model, but to function at production level it was critical to automate our multilayered mold's workflow. The script we developed:

— offsets multiple layers from the positive,

— controls seam placement and alignment so layers can be wrapped around one another and leave no open seams,

— creates a fitted scaffold that resists the load of the slip.

Testing molds generated by the digital workflow revealed how the formwork can create a high degree of control in the specific areas, while allowing other parts to be less rigid without affecting the integrity of an assembly. This in turn informed the design of the screen prototype.

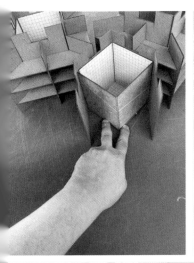

Tests were conducted to determine the adequate casting time and determine the structural integrity of the molds.

The assembly of each mold is easily accomplished since the cardboard can be etched with information that directs the organization of the parts.

We designed the XBlock screen to simulate a small production run of unique components, demonstrate the ability of the system to create precise alignments, and help tighten the parameters of the scaffold script. With these goals in mind, we selected a section of the screen that could be dry-stacked. The run demonstrated that, while traditional mold making techniques have a turnover of several days or even weeks to manufacture and cure, our disposable mold can move from digital model to slip filled mold in a few hours, opening the possibility that the system could be used for affordable scale prototyping if not final production.

In testing, we discovered the necessity of a rigid exterior support for each mold to counter the deformation caused by gravity while flipping the mold for draining. Several alternatives were considered, including a 3d printed exterior shell and custom 3d milled components. To keep the process' waste stream low, we developed a standardized wood frame that would fit all the molds and could be used repetitively.

Each chipboard mold will fit into a standardized wood box to facilitate the removal of excess slip during the casting process.

To augment the potential of the system, the team plans improvements designed to stabilize units while firing and integration of finish patterning into the paper mold. Clay ribs are often added by hand in the factory to provide stability during the drying and firing process. This requires an open form and additional labor, but formwork that produces these internal ribs, could be integrated into the system. These could also help create more intricate forms that benefit from internal support.

Surface finish has a strong effect on expression, so looking at bringing this into the system is paramount. For the XBlock, a colored clay slip was printed onto the surface of the mold material prior to laser cutting. This layer transferred to the cast units, producing a bright blue surface on each block. Professor Hopp is exploring the possibility to print, and laser etch surface designs onto the mold in colored underglazes or glazes. This would integrate glazing into the digital workflow and make it customizable as highly articulated color deposition is made available. Combining casting and glazing reduces production waste and lowers the environmental impact of production making a sustainable product even more ecologically friendly.

After the tissue paper is applied to the chipboard, glaze or slip can be rolled on to the material that will make up the mold.

The XBlock units before and after firing show the potential for color application embedded in the casting process.

The prototype production drew from the varied skillsets of the team to understand the behavior of the mold, systematize the digital workflow, and organize a complex assembly of parts for efficient production. The resulting system moves from digital model to slip cast components with speed and economy, and also represents a reduction of waste and energy use. Looking outside the realm of manufacturing, to the built fabric of our cities, this process expands the form finding potential for architectural terra cotta. It promotes the possibility for manufacturers of these assemblies to deliver aggregations of unique units, which the material's inherent plasticity recommends to the designer's imagination. It also fulfills the promise of digital fabrication—that of endless variation at low cost.

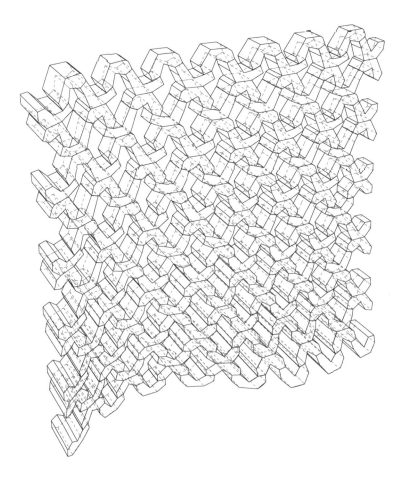

A part of the screen with double curvature was selected for the prototype assembly

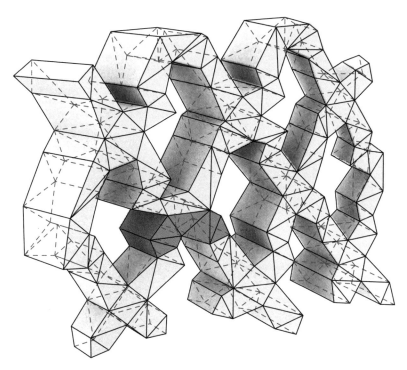

A screen was developed using the CBlock module in which each component was unique, and an area of 20 blocks was selected for prototyping. Two vertical edge blocks were produced to complete the assembly which would not be part of the larger screen.

The prototype assembly demonstrated the possibility of casting a large set of completely unique units.

179

Support
Organizers, Consultants, Speakers

Supporting Institutions

Boston Valley Terra Cotta

Boston Valley Terra Cotta was established by the Krouse family in 1981 following the purchase of Boston Valley Pottery. Utilizing both superior terra cotta engineering knowledge and sculpting talent, Boston Valley Terra Cotta has become one of the leading manufacturers of architectural terra cotta in the country. Boston Valley commenced operations with the restoration of Louis Sullivan's Guaranty Building. Since then, the company has been awarded contracts for some of the most notable buildings around the country. They have over 30 years of experience in design engineering, drafting, model and mold making, clay body and glaze development, and customer service. They operate a facility in Orchard Park, NY with 170,000 square feet of work space and over 150 employees.

The School of Architecture and Planning at the University at Buffalo (SUNY)

The UB School of Architecture and Planning was created in 1968 as a direct challenge to orthodox design education. It lives those original principles today, committed to architecture and planning as interdisciplinary problem-solving enterprises, rooted in social engagement, nourished by research-in-practice, animated by making and doing, and committed to meeting the needs of clients, communities, and society in an increasingly complex urban world.

Throughout nearly half a century of work, the people of the School of Architecture and Planning have grappled with how to make cities more livable and humane; how to conserve and produce energy within the urban fabric; how to make every environment more accessible to people of all abilities; and how to make all of the built environment more responsive to our human goals and protective of our increasingly fragile natural ecologies. In our early years, faculty were inspired by the insights of general systems theorists and the Bauhaus dream of a fusion of technology and art in service to society. Over the years, other intellectual traditions have made their mark on the life of the school. But some things have remained constant even as they have grown and flowered, namely a commitment to research, engaged work, and the values of urbanism.

Walter P Moore is an innovative team of engineers, architects scientists managers, technical specialists,and creative people—driven to solve some of the world's most complex challenges of our time. Working across the globe, the firm included structural engineering, civil and Traffic engineering, urban diagnostics practice, and technology consulting. The people of Walter P Moore have one vision, and that's to see the possibilities in our clients' objectives and make them happen, whatever the challenge. And do this in a manner that's rewarding to all. They have been helping clients this way since 1931.

Organizers

John B. Krouse

President and CEO, Boston Valley Terra Cotta

John Krouse is a Ceramic Engineer and the CEO of Boston Valley Terra Cotta in Orchard Park, NY.

Boston Valley specializes in the manufacturing of historic terra cotta replication, new construction and innovation in contemporary rain screen design and production. John is a graduate of Alfred University with a B.S. in Ceramic Engineering and a minor in Ceramic Sculpture and has over 30 years of experience in terra cotta manufacturing. Boston Valley has successfully completed well over 3,000 building projects with John leading the company. These projects range in size and scope from large government buildings to small private art galleries.

Omar Khan

Head, School of Architecture, Carnegie Mellon University

Co-organizer of the Architectural Ceramics Assemblies Workshop (ACAW)

Omar Khan is Professor and Head of the School of Architecture at Carnegie Mellon University and co-organizer of the Architectural Ceramics Assemblies Workshop (ACAW). Khan was previously an Associate Professor at the University at Buffalo (SUNY) and co-director of the Sustainable Manufacturing and Advanced Robotic

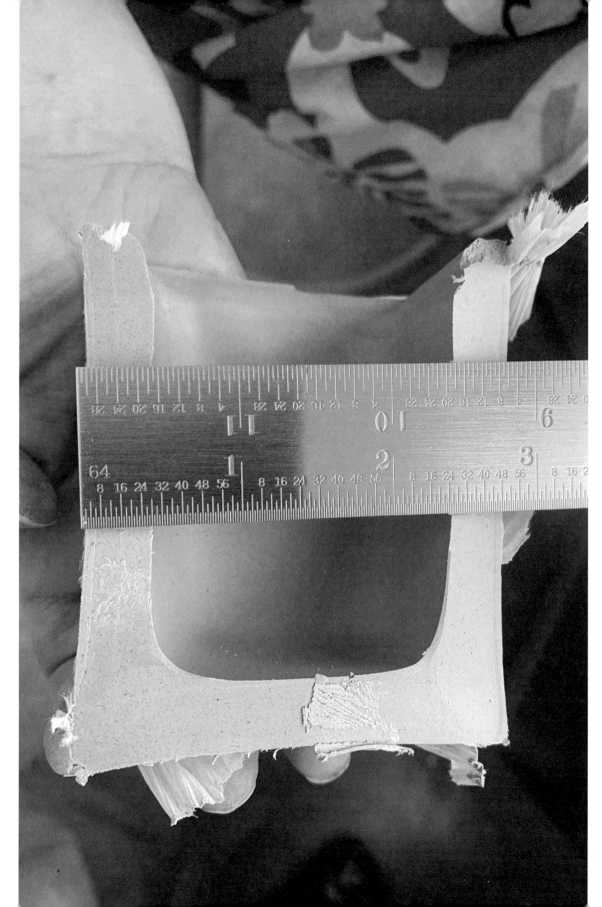

Technologies (SMART) Community of Excellence where he spearheaded academia and industry research partnerships. ACAW is a product of that initiative, a research collaboration supported by Boston Valley Terra Cotta to explore material and design innovations in architectural ceramics. Khan, with his partner Laura Garofalo, also edits the annual books chronicling the research and prototypes developed through ACAW.

Mitchell Bring

Mitchell Bring is an aging enthusiastic proto-hacker with an enduring appreciation of great design. He built his first computers in a garage not far from Cape Canaveral (now called Kennedy Space Center), many years before Steve Jobs got out of diapers. He went to architecture school during the time of punched paper card input, but he did get to study with pioneer thinkers Jim Fitzgibbon and Buckminster Fuller. After living and writing in Japan for several years, then getting his graduate degree from Berkeley, he started the Georgia Tech Architecture CAD Lab with an academic grant of 10 seats of AutoCad 2. Seduced away from academia by the lure of easy money and fast technology, he started and sold a couple of software companies, only to find out, that change in architecture is slow and the money isn't so great either. He remains fascinated by the possibility of building responsive buildings that can respond to the environmental specifics over time; and developing a design and production process that will meet the imagination of those who design buildings and for those who live and work within. He has taught architecture and/or planning at the University of California, Berkeley, Montana State, Georgia Tech, Carnegie Mellon, and the University at Buffalo. At UB, he worked for nine years as an "embedded" faculty mentor at Boston Valley Terra Cotta facilitating change and creating better means for the collaborative creation of architecture.

Together with BVTC President John Krouse and then UB Chair of Architecture Omar Khan, he helped create the Architectural Ceramics Assemblies Workshop and continues on as the workshop coordinator.

Andy Brayman

Matter Factory, Boston Valley Terra Cotta, Glaze Research and Development Specialist

Andy Brayman holds a BA in sociology and a BFA in ceramics from the University of Kansas (1996) and an MFA in ceramics from Alfred

University (1998). His work is a combination of traditional craft, industrial processes, physical computing, and contemporary art strategies. At their best, his pieces demonstrate an object's potential to be both beautiful and cerebral. In 2005, Andy founded The Matter Factory in Kansas City. It is part artist studio, part laboratory, and part factory. In addition to producing objects of his design, Brayman conducts research on glazes and forming methods for Boston Valley Terra Cotta in conjunction with architectural firms.

Consultants

Nat Domst
Color Lab Lead, Boston Valley Terra Cotta

Craig Kacalski
Operations Manager, Boston Valley Terra Cotta

Andrew Pries
Production Manager, Boston Valley Terra Cotta

Peter Schmidt
Information Technology Manager, Boston Valley Terra Cotta

Speakers

Keynote Speaker
James von Klemperer
President, Design Principal, KPF Associates

James von Klemperer is President and Design Principal at Kohn Pedersen Fox Associates where he began as a young architect in 1983. His work ranges in scale from a house to a city, and he contributes closely to these efforts from conception to completion. In addition to focusing on his own projects, he leads the community of designers within the firm in exploring shared architectural agendas and goals. As President of the firm, he is responsible for leading the staff of 650 people in 9 offices around the world.

A major focus of Jamie's work has been to heighten the role that large buildings play in making urban space. He has explored this theme in major projects in Asia including the China Resources Tower in Shenzhen, Plaza 66 and the Jing An Kerry Centre in Shanghai, China Central Place in Beijing, and the 123-story Lotte World Tower in Seoul. In New York, his design for One Vanderbilt will link Midtown's tallest tower directly to Grand Central Terminal. Each of these projects creates strong symbiotic relationships between program space and the public realm. At the larger scale, his design for New Songdo City extends this challenge to the scope of urban planning.

Erik Verboon

Principal, Managing Director NY Office, Director of Enclosure Engineering, Walter P Moore

Erik Verboon is the Co-Founder and Managing Director of Walter P Moore's New York office. Trained in both architecture and engineering, Erik brings a deep global experience with a focus on the design of complex and high-performance building envelopes for a wide range of building types. Erik also has experience working with a wide variety of façade applications including high-performance, double-skin façades, geometrically complex composite façades, and custom unitized enclosures for both new buildings and existing building retrofits and additions.

His experience in digital design, geometric rationalization, and environmental analysis allows him to bring the highest level of value to his clients while also helping designers deliver projects to the highest level of design sophistication while maximizing performance and minimizing cost. Erik's portfolio expresses both national and international work with extensive experience in the New York market, bringing expertise in buildings old and new, across academic, commercial, and cultural sectors. In addition to Erik's professional accolades, he teaches enclosure design at a number of leading universities.

William M. Carty, Ph.D.

John F. McMahon Professor, New York State College of Ceramics at Alfred University

William Carty just retired after 27 years as a professor of ceramic engineering at Alfred University but maintains an active consulting practice. He has worked closely with industry during his tenure at AU generating over $21 million in research funding. He has received numerous teaching awards in ceramic engineering courses and "Ceramic

Science for the Artist" along with industrial short courses. At ACAW he has given lectures on glaze defects, color, out-door ceramic bodies, and energy in terra cotta. He has authored or co-authored over 160 publications, and holds 17 patents (plus nine patents pending).

Roberto Bicchiarelli

Business Development Manager and Lead Concept Designer USA, Permasteelisa North America

Roberto graduated from the University of Rome "La Sapienza" with a degree in Architecture. During his studies, he worked for one of Permasteelisa Group's Italian companies, ultimately in 1991 becoming a Director and a Partner in that business. In 1998, Roberto was asked to join the US operations to contribute as a liaison between the Permasteelisa Group companies and the new American based office overseeing the Sales and Estimating Division with respect to cladding and curtain-wall for monumental buildings.

In 2008 Roberto became General Manager and Sr. Vice President to Permasteelisa North America's Miami-based office. In addition to his General Manager duties, he continues to oversee Sales and Estimating concentrating on the Southern US and Central and South American Markets, while still maintaining a close relation with many of his former projects. From early 2017 Roberto covered the role of Lead Concept Designer and from June 2018 also the role of Business Development Manager of the East Coast. Currently he is working for Gartner USA, a division of Permasteelisa North America.

Susan Knack-Brown

Senior Principal, Simpson Gumpertz & Heger Inc.

Ms. Knack-Brown is a Senior Principal at Simpson Gumpertz & Heger Inc. Her work includes a range of building enclosure investigations and designs involving both contemporary structures and landmarks. Ms. Knack-Brown specializes in large-scale preservation and adaptive reuse projects where she applies technology to the restoration of landmark buildings and works with owners to extend the function and performance of existing buildings. Some of Susan's signature projects include the multi-phase, multi-year roof rehabilitation and skylight restoration on the New York State Capitol, the roof replacement on the Massachusetts State House, and on-going work at The First Church of Christ, Scientist.

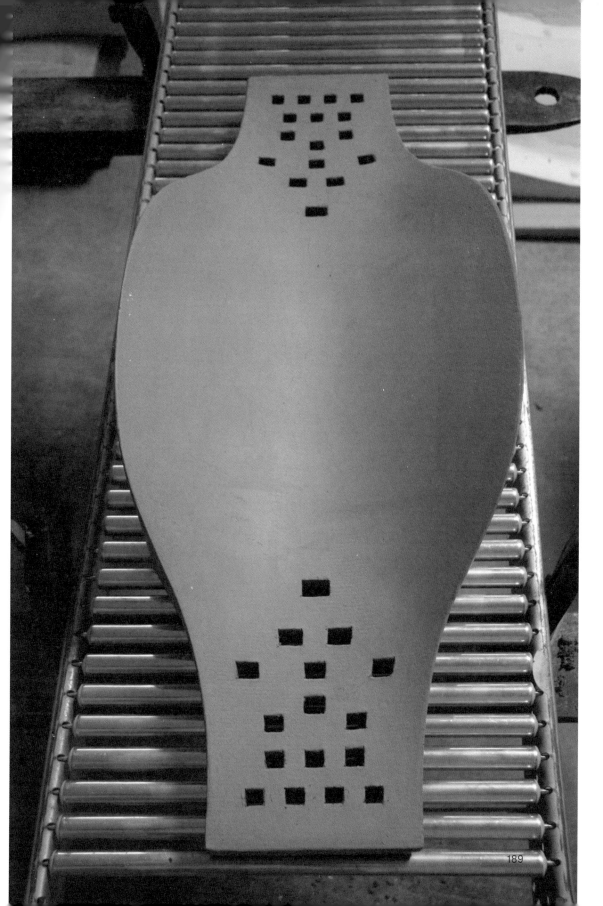

189

Published by Applied Research and Design Publishing, an imprint of ORO Editions.
Gordon Goff: Publisher

www.appliedresearchanddesign.com
info@appliedresearchanddesign.com

Editors: Laura Garófalo and Omar Khan
Editorial assistance: Adam Levin
Book design: Office of Luke Bulman
Project Manager: Jake Anderson

Image credits
Photos in each chapter shot by team members, Boston Valley Terracotta staff, or editors unless otherwise credited
Pages 37, 52, 53,125, 131, 147, 149. courtesy of Boston Valley Terra Cotta, USA ©Julian Ross Imaging 2021.
Page 103. National Aeronautics and Space Administration (NASA).
Page 134. © 2017 Elsevier B.V. All rights reserved.
Page 138. Left: Sue Linday © Australian Museum. Right: © Can Stock Photo / Digifuture.
Page 154. Left: Sue Linday © Australian Museum. Right: © Can Stock Photo/Digifuture.
Page 95. Top: © Can Stock Photo / AndrewChisholm. Bottom © Can Stock Photo/ AndrewChisholm.

10 9 8 7 6 5 4 3 2 1   First Edition

ISBN: 978-1-954081-71-0

Color Separations and Printing: ORO Group Ltd.
Printed in China.

AR+D Publishing makes a continuous effort to minimize the overall carbon footprint of its publications. As part of this goal, AR+D, in association with Global ReLeaf, arranges to plant trees to replace those used in the manufacturing of the paper produced for its books. Global ReLeaf is an international campaign run by American Forests, one of the world's oldest non-profit conservation organizations. Global ReLeaf is American Forests' education and action program that helps individuals, organizations, agencies, and corporations improve the local and global environment by planting and caring for trees.